Medical Toxicology Unit, Guy's & St Thomas' Hospital Trust

Chemical Incident Management for Public Health Physicians

Dr David J Irwin

Dr David T Cromie

Dr Virginia Murray

London: The Stationery Office

Published with the permission of the Department of Health on behalf of the Controller of Her Majesty's Stationery Office

© Crown Copyright 1999

First published 1999

ISBN 0 11 322107 X

Chemical Incident Management for Public Health Physicians

Medical Toxicology Unit
Guy's & St Thomas' Hospital Trust

Chemical Incident Management Series

Other volumes in the series:

Chemical Incident Management Handbook

Chemical Incident Management for Accident and Emergency Clinicians

Contents

Figures

Contributors

Dr David J Irwin graduated in medicine from Queen's University of Belfast in 1986 and started training in Public Health in 1991 in the North Thames Regional Health Authority. His trainee rotations included the London School of Hygiene and Tropical Medicine (where he was awarded an MSc in PHM in 1992), Barking and Havering Health Authority, the Public Health Laboratory Service, the Communicable Disease Surveillance Centre, Chelmsford Public Health Laboratory and North Essex Health Authority. He was admitted to Membership of the Faculty of Public Health Medicine in 1995. He was appointed as part-time Consultant in Communicable Disease Control, initially in Rotherham, January – August 1996, where he managed a community outbreak of meningococcal septicaemia, and then at North Essex Health Authority from September 1996, when he was seconded to the Medical Toxicology Unit where he revised, expanded and updated this book.

Dr David T Cromie is a Consultant with Lanarkshire Health Board. As a Senior Registrar in Public Health Medicine he was attached to the Scottish Centre for Infection and Environmental Health and represented the Scottish Consultants in Public Health Medicine (CD & EH) Working Group in his contribution to this book. He has participated in National Seminars on the management of chemical incidents and water failures. He is currently a member of the Emergency Planning Group, Lanarkshire Health Board and was a member of the Lanarkshire Outbreak Team during the 1996 central Scotland *E.coli* 0157 outbreak. He has particular interests in the public health aspects of waste incineration and elemental mercury.

Dr Virginia Murray trained in occupational medicine before joining the National Poisons Information Service, London, and the Medical Toxicology Unit in 1980. Initially she was involved in projects organised by the Unit and the International Programme on Chemical Safety (WHO/ILO/UNEP). Since 1988 she has played a key role in developing the unit's ability to respond to problems arising from chemical incidents. In 1989, she started the Chemical Incident Research Programme at the unit and is currently the Director of the Chemical Incident Response Service. As a result she has had considerable experience in advising on response to chemical incidents.

Foreword

Major chemical incidents occur infrequently, but the risk is ever present, not just in industrial areas, but from contamination of water supplies or from accidents on the road. Many other incidents can only be defined as 'minor' in retrospect, and may generate considerable public alarm before it is possible to establish that there is no risk to health.

When these incidents occur, the local public health department is called to advise and take action, usually in collaboration with other agencies. However, many public health practitioners feel extremely ill-prepared to deal with such situations. I therefore greatly welcome the publication of this book, which I know will be of enormous assistance to my public health colleagues as well as to other agencies involved in such incidents. It rightly emphasises surveillance, but it also provides excellent practical advice about the management of an incident and a comprehensive list of sources of information and support.

I commend this book to people working in all the agencies which may contribute to the management of chemical incidents. It forms a valuable basis for the preparation and discussion of joint plans as well as a framework for multidisciplinary teamwork, upon which effective public health action depends.

Dr June Crown

Immediate Past President, Faculty of Public Health Medicine

Acknowledgements

The authors wish to thank the following:

Dr Susan Schonfield, Consultant in Public Health Medicine, South Thames Regional Office and Dr Amelia Cummins, Consultant in Communicable Disease Control, South Essex Health Authority with grateful thanks for their inspiration for this book whilst on secondment to the Chemical Incident Response Service and for their work on the first version.

Dr June Crown, Immediate Past President of the Faculty of Public Health Medicine and Director, South East Institute of Public Health

Mr Huw Bowen, Head of National Focus for work on the response to chemical incidents and surveillance of health effects of environmental chemicals, Welsh Combined Centres for Public Health, Cardiff

Dr Peter Christie, Consultant Epidemiologist, Scottish Centre for Infection and Environmental Health

Dr Donald Campbell, Consultant Epidemiologist, Scottish Centre for Infection and Environmental Health, now at Health Protection, Auckland Health Care, New Zealand

Dr Judith Fisher, Consultant Accident and Emergency Physician, Royal London Hospitals Trust, now at the Princess Alexandra Hospital, Harlow

Dr John Harrison, Medical Director, National Radiological Protection Board

Dr Rachel Heathcock, Consultant in Communicable Disease Control, Lambeth, Southwark and Lewisham Health Authority

Mr Stephen Hedley, Principal Environmental Health Officer, South East Institute of Public Health

Medical Toxicology Unit

Henrietta Wheeler, Information Scientist, Chemical Incident Response Service

Joan Bennett, PA to Dr Murray, Chemical Incident Response Service

Nick Edwards, Manager, National Poisons Information Service, London

Alison Dines, Information Scientist, National Poisons Information Service, London

Helaina Checketts, Librarian

Dr Glyn Volans, Director

Members of the Public Health Medicine Environment Group, and many others who have read and commented upon the text.

Authors and publisher are grateful to copyright holders for permission to reproduce the following:

Figure 1, 'Vehicle hazard warning panels', reproduced from *Road Transport Carriage of Dangerous Goods (by Road) Regulations 1996*, HMSO 1996. Figure 2, 'Summary of routes of exposure, absorption, distribution and excretion of toxic chemicals in humans', reproduced from *Substances Hazardous to Health*, ed. Ward Gardner, Croner Publications, 1986, p.1.31.

Abbreviations

ATSDR	Agency for Toxic Substances and Disease Registry – US federal agency
BASICS	British Association for Immediate Care
CAS	Chemical Abstract Series
CCDC	Consultant in Communicable Disease Control
CDC	Centers for Disease Control and Prevention – US epidemiological surveillance organisation
CEAS	Chemical Emergency Agency Service
CEC	Commission of the European Communities
CEHIC	Center for Environmental Health and Injury Control, part of CDC
CEPO	County Emergency Planning Officer
CHEMET	Chemical Incident Meteorological Forecasting Service
CHEMSAFE	Chemical Industry Scheme for Assistance in Freight Emergencies
CHIP	Chemical Hazards Identification and Packaging Regulations
CIMAH	Control of Industrial Major Accident Hazards Regulations
COMAH	Control of Major Accident Hazards Regulations
COSHH	Control of Substances Hazardous to Health Regulations
CPHM	Consultant in Public Health Medicine
DoH	Department of Health (England and Wales)
DHSSNI	Department of Health and Social Services for Northern Ireland
DoE	Department of the Environment
DoENI	Department of the Environment for Northern Ireland
EA	Environment Agency
EHO	Environmental Health Officer
EPCU	Emergency Planning Co-ordination Unit
EPO	Emergency Planning Officer
F&CDA	Fire & Civil Defence Authorities
FEPA	Food & Environmental Protection Act
FHSA	Family Health Services Authority
HAGCCI	Health Advisory Group on Chemical Contamination Incidents
HAZCHEM	Hazardous Chemical

HEPA	Health Emergency Planning Adviser
HEPO	Health Emergency Planning Officer
HSE	Health and Safety Executive
HSG	Health Service Guidance
ICSC	International Chemical Safety Card
IPCS	International Programme on Chemical Substances–(WHO/ILO/UNEP)
LGC	Laboratory of the Government Chemist
MAFF	Ministry for Agriculture, Fisheries & Food
MHIDAS	Major Hazard Incident Data Service – part of AEA Technology plc
MPCU	Marine Pollution Control Unit
MTU	Medical Toxicology Unit
NAIR	National Arrangements for Incidents involving Radioactivity
NATO	North Atlantic Treaty Organisation
NCEC	National Chemical Emergency Centre – part of AEA Technology plc
NEHAP	National Environmental Health Action Plan
NHSE	National Health Service Executive
NIEH	Non-infectious Environmental Hazard
NIHHS	Notification of Installations Handling Hazardous Substances Regulations
NIO	Northern Ireland Office
NPIS	National Poisons Information Service
NRPB	National Radiological Protection Board
NTIS	National Teratology Information Service
ONS	Office for National Statistics
PPE	Personal Protective Equipment
RDPH	Regional Director of Public Health
RIMNET	Radioactive Incident Monitoring Network
SCIEH	Scottish Centre for Infection and Environmental Health
SEIPH	South East Institute of Public Health
SEPA	Scottish Environment Protection Agency
SHHD	Scottish Home and Health Department
SO	Scottish Office

SOAEFD	Scottish Office, Agriculture, Environment and Fisheries Department
SODoH	Scottish Office Department of Health
TREM	Transport Emergency Cards
WHO	World Health Organisation
WMIB	Waste Management Information Bureau, based at AEA Technology plc
WO	Welsh Office

INTRODUCTION

Chemical incidents occur every day and may involve anyone, whether at work or not, in a variety of ways. Health authorities,[1] through their public health departments, have responsibilities for the management of non-infectious environmental hazards (specified in the Abrams Report in 1993, HSG(93)56).[2] Although such incidents occur frequently, involvement of health authorities and public health physicians is rare. As a result, public health physicians have varying levels of experience (and confidence) in dealing with chemical incidents. It is therefore important that incidents are managed in a systematic manner to ensure that any potential damage arising from them is minimised.

This volume in the Chemical Incident Management series seeks to provide support for public health physicians in exercising these responsibilities.

This book identifies four stages in the integrated management approach to major incidents.

1. Prevention

2. Preparedness

3. Response

4. Recovery

A section of the book is devoted to each of these stages, and some more detailed information is given in the appendices.

What is a chemical incident?

There has been a great deal of discussion concerning the definition of a 'chemical incident', depending on a hierarchy of hazards: whether humans are exposed, in what numbers, how severe the exposure is, and whether illness is shown after the exposure.

A useful definition to promote an early public health response is:

An event leading to exposure of two or more individuals to any substance resulting in illness or a potentially toxic threat to health.

This has been modified from a definition given by Hill and O'Sullivan in 1992.[3] It is useful because it encompasses incidents both serious and trivial, enabling identification of severe problems at an earlier stage. It also includes chemicals which may be both toxic and radioactive. While separate, specific rules and regulations apply to such substances, the general principles are similar, and for medical planning purposes they should be considered identical. However, radiation is more easily detected and quantified.

This definition does not distinguish between events that are specifically planned for and those that are not. An example of the former is the Health Authority emergency planning response for incidents involving known agents at industrial sites. In this case, the event should have been anticipated in scenarios prepared under health and safety legislation, and the health authority has a role in the industrial off-site emergency plan for Control of Industrial Major Accident Hazards Regulations (CIMAH) sites.

National Environmental Health Action Plan

The UK National Environmental Health Action Plan (NEHAP)[4] was instigated in response to a commitment to the Second European Conference on Environmental Health which was held in Helsinki in 1994.

The objectives of the NEHAP, as set out in section 3.6, Natural Disasters and Industrial and Nuclear Accidents, are:

'To limit the consequences of natural disasters, prevent the occurrence and limit the consequences of major industrial and nuclear accidents, and ensure the existence of effective arrangements for emergency preparedness for and response to natural and man made disasters, in and between countries.'

'To ensure that the appropriate levels of government and the relevant public services, as well as members of the public, are fully informed of the probability and potential risks of industrial and nuclear accidents, can put those risks into perspective and understand the action required of them in the event of an emergency.'

Section 3.6 also states: *'Further work is needed to develop and inform the public health response to chemical accidents – especially in the context of risk assessment, the rapid availability of expert information and advice to those dealing with the incident at the local level, and consideration of the need for follow-up action.'*

These objectives will obviously have an impact on the public health function of health authorities, and it is hoped that this book and the other volumes in this series will assist with these processes.

---

[1] The term 'health authority' is used in this book to refer to district health authorities in England and Wales, health boards in Scotland, and health and social services boards in Northern Ireland.

[2] Department of Health, Department of the Environment and National Health Service Management Executive (1993) *Public Health: Responsibilities of the National Health Service and the Roles of Others* (HSG (93) 56), London: DoH, DoE, NHSME.

[3] P. Hill and D. O'Sullivan, (1992), *Survey of arrangement for identification and investigation of incidents of acute exposure of the public to toxic substances*, London, NHS Management Executive.

[4] Department of the Environment, Department of Health, and Northern Ireland, Scottish and Welsh Offices (1996) UKNEHAP, Cm 3323, July, London: HMSO.

Section One

Prevention

Chemical incident management seeks to identify hazards through surveillance, and to institute appropriate preventive measures. Chemical incidents may be rare events for local health authorities, but they can cause significant distress, both to individuals and communities. A rapid and effective response is essential to prevent or minimise chemical exposure which may lead to adverse health effects (of acute or delayed onset) and to prevent or minimise distress.

1 Surveillance

'Surveillance' may be defined as the systematic collection, monitoring, analysis and dissemination of data, which may then be used:

- to describe patterns of diseases and events and to detect changes in these patterns
- to direct investigation, prevention and control activities
- to evaluate prevention and control programmes
- to plan services and allocate resources
- to identify training and education requirements

HSG(93)56 specifically mentions the need for surveillance, including that of longer-term chemical hazards.[1] A surveillance scheme to collect data nationally via chemical incident provider units and other agencies started in April 1998. It is being co-ordinated by the National Focus for Work on Response to Chemical Incidents and Surveillance of the Health Effects of Environmental Chemicals, Cardiff.[2] A report on this work should become available on the first year's data. This surveillance of non-infectious environmental hazards, including chemical incidents, means there will be support for health authorities and their public health departments which are attempting to fulfil their responsibilities in this area.

Surveillance of non-infectious environmental hazards may produce information which will allow health authorities, public health physicians and other organisations to identify areas of concern and ways to optimise the response to incidents, which should ultimately improve public health. Without this information, it is difficult to plan a co-ordinated response and learn lessons from experience.

Although surveillance has been performed in some areas, including the West Midlands, Wales and London, in most areas no systematic surveillance has been carried out. There is therefore little information about the frequency and type of incidents, the substances involved, numbers of people exposed, numbers of people who become unwell, and measures taken in the immediate response to different hazards. Without this knowledge, it is difficult to identify preventive measures.

The value of surveillance in this respect has been demonstrated in the United States, where the Hazardous Substances Emergency Events Surveillance system identified for the first time that emergency personnel (responders) were the group most often suffering health effects as a result of exposure to non-infectious environmental hazards. Such information could then be used to target education programmes and institute safe procedures for these personnel.

In the past, there has been little pooling and co-ordination of data between agencies. If only one source of information is available, it is impossible to produce a complete picture of an incident. In 1994, the All Wales Environmental Health Surveillance Project found that only 10% of incidents notified to its surveillance scheme were reported by more than one organisation.[3] Any surveillance system must therefore include data from a number of different sources in order to include as many different incidents as possible.

A surveillance system for non-infectious environmental hazards, including chemical incidents, should aim:

- to describe the frequency, distribution and nature of incidents
- to describe the health effects experienced by different groups exposed to hazardous substances
- to identify risk factors associated with morbidity and mortality
- to develop strategies to reduce morbidity and mortality
- to identify ways in which the response of all the organisations involved can be improved
- to identify areas where education and training is required

Effective surveillance leads to prevention.

[1] Department of Health, Department of the Environment and National Health Service Management Executive (1993) *Public Health: Responsibilities of the National Health Service and the Roles of Others* (HSG(93)56), London: DoH, DoE, NHSME, p.9.

[2] Department of Health (1997) *National Focus for Work on Response to Chemical Incidents and Surveillance of the Health Effects of Environmental Chemicals*, London: DoH; and Chief Medical Officer (1997) *National Focus for Work on Response to Chemical Incidents and Surveillance of Health Effects of Environmental Chemicals: CMO Update 14*. Further information on the work of this group can be obtained from Huw Bowen, National Focus, Faculty of Community Health Sciences, University of Wales Institute, Cardiff (UWIC), Western Avenue, Cardiff CF5 2YB.

[3] Welsh Office (1995) All Wales Environmental Health Surveillance Project. *Welsh Health: Annual Report of the Chief Medical Officer for Wales*, Cardiff: WO.

Section Two

Preparedness

The preparedness phase – the period before an incident happens – involves setting up an efficient system for emergency response, rehabilitation and follow-up, influenced by experience from previous incidents and/or training sessions. During this phase decisions can be made by consensus.

2 Health service guidance

England and Wales

In England and Wales, the district health authority's role in emergency planning is specified in *Planning for Major Incidents: The NHS Guidance,*[1] revised by the NHSE in November 1998. This document reinforces the guideline document on the public health function, HSG(93)56,[2] and provides extensive guidance on dealing with accidents or incidents involving radioactivity or chemicals and also the district health authority's responsibilities, many of which will be fulfilled through the contracting process. The new document states:

Essential actions

The health authority must:

- ensure that satisfactory plans are developed and maintained for the health authority response to a chemical incident, within the general framework of existing local emergency planning arrangements
- participate in the strategic and tactical management of a chemical incident
- ensure that designated staff are available on a 24-hour basis to respond to a chemical incident
- ensure that such staff are prepared for their roles, through the provision of appropriate training programmes
- designate an individual(s) responsible for ensuring that:
    - the health authority has access to the necessary advice and expertise concerning public health hazards arising from chemical incidents
    - agreements exist with acute hospital trusts, ambulance trusts and other trusts responsible for managing primary and community care, for the provision of an effective health service response in the event of a chemical incident
    - appropriate chemical incident plans are drawn up by such health service trusts, within the general framework of existing local emergency planning arrangements
    - relevant liaison arrangements are formulated in advance, with the other response agencies, including local authority environmental health departments, for the provision of advice on the public health implications of chemical incidents, including clean-up operations
- identify and make available suitable and sufficient resources to ensure that the health authority itself and all health service trusts are able to fulfil their planning and response roles

Communications with the Regional Office/National Focus

The health authority will also be responsible for:

- liaising with the regional office (normally the Regional Director of Public Health (RDPH)) in considering the declaration of a 'Regional Chemical Incident'

The latter has been traditionally defined as one in which:

- more than one health authority is involved, or
- the number of casualties necessitates the need for special provision, or
- the need for specialist advice is such that the RDPH feels that a 'Regional Chemical Incident' should be declared

• notifying the Regional Office Communications Unit, in accordance with the criteria for incident reporting established by the regional office

• alerting and briefing the National Focus (acting on behalf of the Department of Health) in the event of an incident which may either be unusual, particularly complex, likely to have a major impact on public health, likely to attract national media attention or span regional boundaries.

Scotland

In Scotland the health board's role in emergency planning is specified in *Emergency Planning Guidance to the Scottish Health Service*.[3] Health boards have made reference to the HSG documents mentioned above, but these have no legal standing in Scotland. The Shields Report requires health boards to: *'safeguard the public health by controlling outbreaks of communicable disease, identify adverse environmental factors and initiate action to control these, and emergency planning.*[4]

Northern Ireland

In Northern Ireland, the health and social services board's role in emergency planning is specified in *The Emergency Planning Manual for Health and Personal Social Services in Northern Ireland*.[5]

---

[1] National Health Service Executive (1998) *Planning for Major Incidents: The NHS Guidance*, HSC 1998/197, London: NHSE.

[2] Department of Health, Department of the Environment and National Health Service Management Executive (1993) *Public Health: Responsibilities of the National Health Service and the Roles of Others*, HSG(93)56, London: DoH, DoE, NHSME.

[3] Scottish Home and Health Department (1990) *Emergency Planning: Guidance to the Scottish Health Service*, Edinburgh: SHHD.

[4] Scottish Office Department of Health (1996) *Commissioning Better Health: Report of the Short Life Working Group on the Roles and Responsibilities of Health Boards*; Edinburgh: SODoH, p11.

[5] Department of Health and Social Services Northern Ireland (1991) *The Emergency Planning Manual for Health and Personal Social Services in Northern Ireland*; Belfast: DHSSNI. See also DHSSNI (1995), *Arrangements to Deal with Health and Personal Social Services: Aspects of Chemical Contamination Incidents*, Belfast: DHSSNI.

3 Public health roles and responsibilities

The NHS is not the lead agency in managing chemical incidents. Its response forms part of the developing integrated (or seamless) approach to all incidents by the emergency services and statutory authorities.

District level

National Health Service Executive Circular HSC 1998/197 stipulates that in England and Wales, district health authorities must have adequate arrangements for dealing with chemical accidents and that there must be a designated individual responsible for ensuring that appropriate plans are prepared for the district. In the majority of cases, this individual is the consultant in communicable disease control but in some districts there are different arrangements. The designated individual has an important role to play in inter-agency networking, as part of the health authority emergency response team.

Regional level

The health emergency planning adviser is responsible for overall emergency planning at regional level and is the primary inter-agency liaison person. At present, every regional office in England and Wales has a health emergency planning adviser who is responsible for co-ordinating district health authority NHS emergency plans within and across regional boundaries, and where applicable across territorial boundaries. A chemical leak from a tanker travelling along the M6 and M1 in 1995 involved three of the new regional offices, highlighting the need for cross-boundary co-ordination of plans and information-sharing.

Some health emergency planning advisers were initially employed when there were more extensive civil defence plans for health authorities, and some have an armed services background, but in 1991 the Home Secretary reviewed the civil defence arrangements in the light of improved East–West relations, and an approach called 'Integrated Emergency Management' was developed through the Civil Defence Regulations 1993. The result is that health emergency planning advisers' civil defence role has been curtailed, and they are now more involved with planning for chemical and nuclear incidents. They are at present accountable to the regional directors of public health and thus to the chief executives. With the changing role of regions, some regional health emergency planning advisers, for example in South Thames, have moved to district level, taking a leading role from there. It is clear that each regional office will develop a distinctive approach to the issue.

National level

Health emergency planning advisers receive policy guidance from the Emergency Planning Control Unit (EPCU) of the Department of Health. In addition, the EPCU provides a spectrum of policy guidance to other divisions of the NHS, other government departments, the ambulance service, the voluntary sector, the military and UK-based US and NATO forces.

Public health activities

The following is an attempt to identify key public health activities. It is not an exhaustive list and may omit elements important at a local level.

- Hazard identification
  - To establish and maintain an inventory of potential risk sources such as hazardous installations (CIMAH and non-CIMAH sites, nuclear facilities) and transport routes
- Health care provision
  - to identify and, if appropriate, contract with a source of authoritative toxicology advice for chemical incidents
  - to assess the decontamination facilities available, both NHS and non-NHS-based
  - to undertake an inventory of antidotes to known hazards within the district
  - to acquire the necessary equipment and supplies, and to make arrangements to obtain these at short notice
- Planning
  - to draft health authority emergency response guidelines
  - to review plans of local provider units (including the ambulance service) in conjunction with regional health emergency planning advisers
  - to review local installation on-site and off-site plans, liaising with the county/local authority emergency planning officer
  - to decide whether a contingency fund is required
- Contracting
  - to ensure that health authority contracts with provider units cover major incidents, including chemical incidents
- Networking
  - to establishment a chain of command and a network of co-operating response services and experts
  - to run collaborative inter-agency training sessions
- Exercising (testing plans)
  - to test health authority incident plans by means of simulation, table-top or full-scale exercises
  - to participate in multi-agency simulation, table-top or full-scale exercises of emergency plans
- Follow-up
  - to identify sources of expert epidemiological advice
  - to audit real-life incidents to inform and improve the planning and commissioning processes
  - to audit exercises (both health authority and multi-agency) to strengthen alliances and to inform and improve the planning and commissioning processes

4 Relationships with other agencies

A variety of agencies may be involved in dealing with chemical incidents. These have been referred to only briefly above. This chapter provides a fuller explanation of each of the different agencies, detailing their responsibilities and likely roles, but is not necessarily exhaustive.

Emergency services

Police

The police are likely to be the first service alerted during a serious chemical incident. Their main responsibilities are control and co-ordination (apart from an area where a fire is taking place) to ensure the protection and preservation of life and property (including securing and making a site safe, although this function is frequently delegated to the fire service). The control functions relate, in particular, to the general public, both at the incident scene and in the surrounding area, including advising, warning or evacuating those who may be endangered. The co-ordination functions involve liaison with the other emergency services, including providing communications, maintaining access/egress, assisting in dealing with casualties, etc.

The police are also responsible for advising the local authority, requesting assistance from the back-up services and also serving the coroner. The chief constable of a constabulary carries overall responsibility for police actions.

Fire service

The primary responsibility of the fire service is to deal with emergencies involving fire. In these situations, they take charge. They will attend chemical incidents which do not involve a fire, although these may fall outside their statutory authority, so a charge for attendance may be levied.

Apart from protecting life and property during a fire, their role may include rescue, providing advice on dangers and evacuation in connection with dangerous substances, requesting local authority assistance and decontaminating/treating spillages.

Ambulance service

Although it is part of the NHS, the ambulance service is an emergency service and is therefore included in this section. Its primary role is to advise on and co-ordinate medical provision at the site of an emergency, attending to immediate medical needs and subsequently transporting any injured persons to their designated treatment centres. The ambulance service will liaise with medical incident officers, who may be called out if there are many casualties.

There have been difficulties in many areas as a result of a tendency for the other emergency services to view the ambulance service as the only NHS input during the planning for and response to an incident. While the ambulance service can act as an interface with all the other NHS organisations, public health departments must take the lead in planning the response to any incident within their own health authority.

Local government

Local government in the UK is arranged into three tiers:

- the district tier , which includes district, borough and some smaller city councils
- the county tier
- the new unitary authorities – multi-purpose authorities undertaking both district and county functions

It is worth noting that the boundaries of health authorities and local authorities may not be coterminous. This may result in a local authority having to work with more than one health authority and vice versa.

A discussion of the nature of local government and its functions is beyond the scope of this volume, other than to point out that most of the functions undertaken are statutory, but non-statutory functions account for many of the main differences between local authorities, particularly where they provide services on an agency basis for other authorities.

The main role for local authorities in dealing with civil emergencies and chemical incidents – particularly if they are large-scale incidents – is to complement the activities of the emergency services. Their other important roles include pre-incident planning (where the local authority takes a leading role), organising simulation exercises, establishing evacuation and reception centres, providing social work advice and assistance, post-incident counselling, clearing up after the incident and law enforcement.

Key local authority personnel include county emergency planning officers, environmental health officers, housing department and social services department staff.

Other agencies

This list is not exhaustive but indicates the wide range of agencies which may have a role during a chemical incident.

Environment Agency/Scottish Environment Protection Agency

The Environment Agency (EA) is a regulatory body that has been formed by combining the National Rivers Authority, Her Majesty's Inspectorate of Pollution and the Waste Regulatory Authority in England and Wales. In Scotland, the Scottish Environment Protection Agencey (SEPA) fulfills the same role. Both the EA and SEPA have statutory responsibilities in connection with pollution of the air, land, and inland and coastal waters, and routinely deal with chemical incidents, particularly those involving water and land. Specific response times following notification of an incident to the agencies have been set, and memoranda of understanding have been drawn up between these and other agencies. Liaison and advice may be available following incidents including those involving radiation.

Health and Safety Executive

The role of the Health and Safety Executive (HSE) is to inspect, investigate and prosecute offenders under the Health and Safety at Work Act 1974. The HSE may be able to offer technical advice and support to the emergency services in their response to contain a hazard and minimise the risk to the public.

Ministry of Agriculture, Fisheries and Food/Scottish Office Agriculture, Environment and Fisheries Department

The Ministry of Agriculture, Fisheries and Food (MAFF) and the Scottish Office Agriculture, Environment and Fisheries Department (SOAEFD) are responsible for ensuring that food is safe for human consumption. These organisations can provide advice on the impact of chemical and radiological contamination on foodstuffs both vegetable and animal, and they work closely with the Department of Health or the Scottish Office Department of Health on all aspects of food contamination.

National Radiological Protection Board

The National Radiological Protection Board (NRPB) is responsible for providing information and advice to persons including government departments and health professionals regarding the protection of the community as a whole, or sub-groups within it, from radiological hazards. Advice is available on the hazards, environmental impact and risks to individuals which may arise as a consequence of an accident or incident involving ionising radiation. Many substances exhibit both radioactive and chemical toxic effects. The NRPB is also responsible for the co-ordination of the National Arrangements for Incidents involving Radioactivity (NAIR), under which local police forces can seek assistance, advice and monitoring of radiation from competent authorities during any incident. (Information on NAIR is available from the NRPB.)

Chemical Incident Response Services

Health authorities should have a chemical incident advisory service. In the UK a number of providers of this service operate. In England and Wales and Northern Ireland health authorities should ensure that there is a contract with a provider. Providers include:

Centre for Chemical Incidents, Institute of Public Health and Epidemiology, University of Birmingham

Chemical Incident Management Support Unit, University of Wales Institute, Cardiff

Chemical Incident Response Service, Medical Toxicology Unit, Guy's and St Thomas' Hospital, London

Department of Environmental & Occupational Medicine and Epidemiology & Public Health, University of Newcastle, Newcastle upon Tyne

Scottish Centre for Infection and Environmental Health

The Scottish Centre for Infection and Environmental Health serves the public health community in Scotland. Under the NHS, it delivers an advice and support service, surveillance, education and training, and undertakes research on environmental and infection issues, including chemical incidents.

National Focus for Chemical Incidents

The National Focus started in January 1997 with a remit to support NHS national surveillance, promote suitable training and undertake general co-ordination in promoting a consistent NHS response and approach to chemical incidents. It also has a remit to alert the Department of Health and activate the Health Advisory Group on Chemical Contamination Incidents (HAGCCI).

Health Advisory Group on Chemical Contamination Incidents

The terms of reference of HAGCCI are to advise on request, urgently if necessary, any department of public health in the UK and the chief medical officers of the UK in the event of an incident leading to chemical contamination transmitted through environmental pathways (air, soil or water) which might affect health or cause public concern on health grounds, including:

- the extent to which illness occurring in the area following the incident may be attributable to the toxic properties of the contaminating chemicals
- the likelihood of prolonged or delayed health effects
- any diagnostic or therapeutic measures which should be offered to those affected, or to the whole population of the area
- any epidemiological, clinical or other investigations required to determine the nature and extent of exposure of members of the public, body burdens or pollutants, and effects
- any long-term health surveillance required

HAGCCI consists of an advisory panel of approximately 60 experts. Since being established in 1991, HAGCCI has been activated only once.

While HAGCCI's remit is confined to larger-scale incidents with major public health implications, it needs information in order to brief ministers and respond to media enquiries. Since the introduction of the National Focus, responsibility for the activation of HAGCCI has passed to the National Focus.

CHEMET

This scheme is operated by the Meteorological Office, providing advice to the emergency services in the event of a release of toxic substances.

CHEMSAFE

This is the UK chemical industry response scheme to provide rapid expert advice and support to the emergency services in the event of an emergency during the distribution of chemicals.

The Armed Forces

Due to their breadth of experience in dealing with crisis situations, and their training in nuclear, chemical and biological warfare, liaison with local military personnel to foster links may prove helpful to health authorities.

The Royal Mail

This is the only agency that can identify every property within any given post code and would be actively involved in the distribution of written emergency advice to the public, possibly as a special delivery.

Voluntary organisations

Many of these organisations will have links to local authority social services departments and county emergency planning officers and can undertake support functions during an incident:

British Red Cross

St John Ambulance / St Andrew's Ambulance

British Association for Immediate Care

Women's Royal Voluntary Service / Scottish Women's Royal Voluntary Service

Women's Institute

Addresses and contact details of government departments, agencies and other organisations can be found in Appendix 1.

5   Health authority chemical incident plans

The health authority chemical incident plan (which may be based on the health authority's emergency plan) should provide a framework for responding to a chemical incident irrespective of its nature and be capable of operation by all public health physicians involved in the on-call rota.

In England and Wales, the challenge of devising a plan is to encapsulate the principles set out in HSC(1998)197 within a framework of local operational procedures.[1] Currently, few of these plans have been tested. One of the most important issues to be addressed is that of notification of an incident to a health authority: agreement will have to be reached with the emergency services on the most appropriate method.

Contents of current plans

A district chemical incident plan should briefly cover each of the following:

- **Background**
  - explanation of the role of the health authority
  - roles and responsibilities of the agencies involved
  - definition of an incident
- **Obtaining all relevant information possible**
  - details of the incident, chemicals involved, exposures and health effects (a sample chemical incident inquiry form can be found in Appendix 3)
- **Trigger events for the plan**
  - criteria for declaring an incident
- **Checklist of actions**
  - risk assessment
  - action in the event of a minor incident
  - action in the event of a major incident
  - action in the event of a regional or national incident
  - forming a health response team, defining the terms of reference of this team and key and co-opted membership
  - arrangements for disseminating public information, media liaison and provision of counselling to rescue workers and the public
  - publishing action cards
- **Arrangements for exceptional circumstances**
  - health care delivery at evacuation centres
  - provision of temporary mortuary/body-holding areas
- **Criteria for declaring an incident over**
- **Arrangements for follow-up of exposed individuals**
- **List of local, regional and national contacts**

– this should include out-of-hours telephone numbers (a list of sources of information is given in Appendix 1)

- **Footnotes**
  – guidance on specific problems, e.g. water, food, air, nuclear contamination, investigation of a chemical incident

Exercises

Health authority plans should be tested during regular exercises, which should involve all key staff likely to participate in an incident response. Such exercises enable the health authority to judge whether the plans function effectively, and identifiy problem areas which require remedial action.

Health authorities should also participate actively in multi-agency emergency planning exercises. This facilitates networking and identification of problem areas or misunderstandings between agencies.

[1] National Health Service Executive (1998) *Planning for Major Incidents: The NHS Guidance*, HSC 1998/197, London: NHSE.

6 Response Team

Creation and membership

When a significant incident is declared, a local response team may need to be formed to investigate the toxic hazards and risks and to co-ordinate countermeasures. One of the functions of this team is to provide public health advice. Mechanisms for providing this advice vary throughout the country: it may be obtained directly from the response team or via a sub-group of it. Public health advice should be drawn up following consultation between key professional groups, including:

public health consultant in communicable disease control/consultant in public health medicine, director of public health

Local authority environmental health officer

county/district emergency planning officers

ambulance service representatives

fire service representatives

police representatives

press officer

clerical support

The group providing public health advice should be able to obtain further information from a variety of individuals, including:

accident and emergency consultant (provider unit)

consultant physician

medical toxicologist

health authority manager

nursing officer

regional epidemiologist/Scottish Centre for Infection and Environmental Health

MAFF/SOAEFD

EA/SEPA

water companies

occupational health physicians

legal advisers

Terms of reference

Given the stress of responding to an acute incident it is essential that public health advice is drawn up in a structured manner. Agreed terms of reference should be available before an incident. These should include consideration of the following issues:

• agreeing and assigning responsibilities

- stressing the confidentiality of information
- establishing an incident room in a health authority/local authority building (this may supplement the police local emergency centre)
- arrangements to co-opt other members as appropriate
- identifying a single spokesperson for the team
- reviewing the evidence to date – toxicological, epidemiological, environmental
- determining level of resources required – staff/financial
- agreeing requirements for media information
- minuting meetings and agreeing actions
- monitoring progress
- agreeing that all decisions should pass through the committee
- agreeing on further investigations
- agreeing case definition
- case-finding/case register
- interviewing cases and collecting data
- evaluating exposure histories
- descriptive epidemiology
- hypothesis-formation
- analytical epidemiology
- assessing the need for long-term follow-up and further biological sampling
- assessing the need for psychological support
- ownership of data
- producing a final report
- auditing the management of the incident
- making recommendations about future plans
- making recommendations about future training requirements for those involved in response
- agreeing authorship for any subsequent publications

7 Communication

One of the most critical factors in responding to a chemical incident is communication, but no single agency in the UK has overall responsibility for co-ordinating this aspect of the response. It is essential that all agencies involved in incident responses liaise with each other and participate in joint exercises regularly, to ensure that any communication problems within the individual organisation and with other agencies are identified and remedied.

Good communications will also help to ensure that each organisation is informed about an incident at an early stage. If this notification comes from a number of allied agencies, so much the better.

Each agency should draw up procedures in advance for communicating within the organisation and with allied agencies, the public and the media.

Within the organisation

The need for rapid communication between health authority personnel, both outside and inside the health authority headquarters, means that a specific room, with a number of computer and telephone points which can receive direct-dialled calls (or can quickly be set up to do so) is likely to be necessary. These telephone numbers must be kept secure for emergency use only. Although mobile telephones can provide an effective means of communication during an incident, the need for confidentiality must be borne in mind (analogue phones can be tapped; digital phones are more secure). Arrangements whereby emergency services can request that non-essential users are temporarily disconnected must be considered especially as many health authorities may not be identified by the emergency services as essential users. Similar arrangements exist for British Telecom terrestrial lines and will require further investigation via the regional health emergency planning adviser.

With allied agencies

Regular routine contact with allied agencies will help improve communication and may allow alternative communication methods to be used during an incident. Systems should enable the establishment of rapid and secure communication links with allied agencies, including health service professionals. It may prove necessary to identify a second room with dedicated telephone lines for this purpose. These numbers should not be divulged to anyone outside the allied agencies. Ideally, a member of the health authority should be an active member of the local response team directly connecting with the arrangements established to ensure communications within each organisation.

With the public

Handling the press is an integral part of incident management procedure and the public appetite for information should not be underestimated.

Parker and Baldwin provide a helpful account of warning the public in an emergency. They note that in an emergency, communication via local radio and television reaches only 51% of the population.[1] There is a need for regular reappraisal of methods for contacting the elderly and those living alone.

It is vital to start providing information as soon as possible. One of the best ways of reducing psychological morbidity is to provide the public with adequate and credible information in a structured way.

CIMAH regulations stipulate that a siren should be sounded to alert the public to an incident but this applies only to CIMAH sites where the public has been pre-warned of the action to be taken.

Parker and Baldwin suggest that in other circumstances where the health of the public is at risk the warning needs to be given with similar speed. They describe three warning periods, starting from when the population is first put at risk (not from when the event is discovered): 0–2 hours, 2–12 hours and 12–24 hours. The warning method depends on the warning period.

First period (0–2 hours)

Initially word of mouth is the only means available, involving as many agencies as possible.

The initiating authority will declare a major emergency and inform the three primary support agencies – police, health and the media. A health service/health authority nominee should be identified in the major incident plan.

The statutory authorities and other agencies have a network of contacts which can be used to disseminate the information from the centre. All other available networks should be used, e.g. the county emergency planning units for county councils and environmental health officers for district council departments. Another example of a network is a local government 'red alert' system, where district and local councils have agreed and named parish 'good neighbours' who know whom to alert. Remember that GPs and district nurses are in the front line and need information to be supplied to them quickly.

Second period (2–12 hours)

The media will still be involved in issuing up-to-date information. All agencies will be receiving phone calls from the public and it is essential that all agencies have the same briefing sheet to ensure consistent information is given out.

There will be time during this period to start preparing and distributing leaflets to the affected population. As many as possible of the agencies already identified should agree the contents of the leaflet and can be used to distribute pre-printed picture leaflets or cards to individuals in the affected area. This must be co-ordinated by a central authority, nominated at the time, to ensure that there are no gaps in the contents of the leaflet or its distribution.

Third period (12–24 hours)

During this period each household and commercial establishment should receive a written communication giving details of the event, the action to be taken by the population and the action being taken by the statutory authorities to ensure a return to normality.

Once the area has been defined by postcodes, the Royal Mail is the only agency that can identify every property in the area and deliver the letters. A special delivery can be organised at any time.

End of incident

A further written communication should be delivered to the affected population but this time by a normal mail delivery.

Helpline

During an incident it may prove necessary for a health authority to institute a public helpline. Arrangements for deciding when to open and how to institute a helpline should be in place prior to an incident.[2]

A room will need to be identified in advance and arrangements must be in place for health authority staff to be seconded to work on the helpline. Consideration will need to be given to the information which will be available to the public over the helpline and mechanisms to enable commonly asked questions to be identified and passed to the public health department so that standard answers can be provided to staff on the helpline. Systems for passing non-standard or difficult callers to senior health authority staff should also be developed. Staff who may be required to work on such a helpline will require training to prepare for this task and frequent debriefing.

Risk communication

The exchange of risk information between public health physicians and affected parties is frequently hampered by differences in the understanding or interpretation of many words and phrases. The technical meaning of much of the terminology used by doctors may differ from colloquial meanings, resulting in confusion. For example, the word 'risk' can have a variety of meanings in different contexts, and there may be difficulties conveying the notions of 'safety' versus 'zero risk' and 'probability'. The mixed messages of 'significant' versus 'non-significant', 'negative' versus 'positive' results, 'population risk' versus 'individual risk', 'relative risk' versus 'absolute risk' and 'association' versus 'causation' can range from mild confusion to a completely contrary interpretation of these words and concepts.

Uncertainties should be avoided wherever possible. If available data are temporarily limited, this may be difficult and uncertainties over interpretations are possible. If information is complex, there may be a problem in understanding what is meant by 'threshold levels', 'measured concentrations' etc.

The media

If the flow of information to the media is poor and the press subsequently report that they cannot establish details, the public may think that not enough is being done, that the services are not coping or that there is a 'cover-up'. Perceived incompetence can result in long-term financial, social and psychological consequences.

The health authority chemical incident adviser should be able to assist in providing briefing material for press conferences on chemical incidents.

Dakin (1994) has provided a useful guide for dealing with the media during an incident, and identifies a number of important elements which contribute to successful media relations.[3]

Press room

A room to be used exclusively for media briefings needs to be identified in advance. Ideally this should be away from areas where health authority work on the incident is taking place. Well-trained press officers from all agencies are required. They will need to work together feeding information to the press in the press room. One of the press officers may be given responsibility for co-ordinating the work of the others.

Designated press liaison officer

A single press spokesperson, who will provide the majority of the media information, should be identified at an early stage by the local response team. This individual may require a member of the health authority to speak directly to the media on occasions. A member of staff prepared to do this should be identified in advance – someone with authority, a strong persuasive personality and the ability to present information to the press with conviction. Close liaison between public health physicians and the health authority media or communications department is essential. Training in speaking to the media should be provided to key members of the health authority on a regular basis.

During a recent chemical disaster, the local community started expressing their fears to the media before the epidemiological response swung into action, and public health credibility suffered as a result. People will look for information, often from the media, when the official information is late, incorrect, ambiguous or full of jargon. Journalists are not well equipped to assess the complexity of chemical incidents and may create fears that no amount of subsequent truthful reassurance can assuage.

If the event is very newsworthy, the press will not only want daily press conferences, but also 'exclusives'. Press access may require firm control; a consistent approach by all agencies is vital, and press attention should not be permitted to inhibit the work of the incident team.

When speaking to the media:

- Come to an interview with two or three key points you want to present to the public. If necessary, repeat them several times during the interview. Each key point should take the form of a 15 to 30 second 'sound bite' suitable for direct use.

- Assume that the interviewer and the target audience have no background knowledge.

- Avoid jargon. Stories must be easy to listen to or easy to read. If you present a simple message, it is less likely to be edited and thereby distorted.

- Avoid gimmicks. They may lead to media exposure, but the gimmick tends to be remembered rather than the message.

- Always have a press release prepared which sets out the facts, e.g. the number of cases, the types of illnesses, the nature of studies being carried out and the public health message you wish to get across.

- Stay within the limits of your expertise. Avoid any speculation. Be prepared to refer an issue to a specialist, if necessary.

- Be prepared for questions that you would prefer not to answer. Tell the truth, but avoid speculation or giving gratuitous information.

Regular press briefings

Journalists need a supply of good new information from press conferences or written press releases. Information should be supplied in time for daily and evening papers' deadlines.

In an incident lasting more than twenty-four hours, it is important to issue a news bulletin or radio broadcast about the incident at the same time each day, so that local people know when to tune in and the press know that regular bulletins are provided. If possible, try organising supervised picture opportunities of the disaster scene, otherwise the press may decide to use ingenuity to get their material.

Ignoring the press can impede services

Journalists will become frustrated if there is a lack of regular incident information and they may forage for themselves to seek information and pictures. The need to do this may be presented to and perceived by the public as a lack of urgency on the part of officials or evidence of a cover-up. Journalists may harass staff in incident rooms and impede rescue operations. In dealing with media representatives, there is a need to supply prompt and accurate information and photo-opportunities.

One solution is to set up a pooling system in the early stages of an incident, whereby two photographers provide material for their colleagues, with a press point where accurate information can be given quickly and regularly (the media are familiar with pooling arrangements, which apply to royal visits). Journalists are then guaranteed some material.

Vehicles for communication

- daily meetings
- newsletters
- local press
- radio broadcasts
- GPs
- town halls/ local authority officials

Monitoring press reports

It is important to monitor radio and television reports by the emergency services to see how the information supplied is being used, and to enable early correction of any misleading lines of press interpretation or scare stories.

Privacy

Your private address/es and phone number/s, and those of your chief executive, should be ex-directory. Ensure that the press officer has the use of a mobile phone during the incident.

Using the media

As mentioned above, the media not only inform the public of what has happened, but can also give help when needed, such as broadcasting appeals for drivers with four-wheel-drive vehicles, catering volunteers, or even blood donors. The press will give out emergency telephone numbers for relatives and friends to call. This can prevent large numbers arriving on the scene to check for themselves or jamming organisations' switchboards.

Litigation

Never agree to interviews with solicitors who represent local residents or industry. Always seek advice from the health authority's solicitors.

Technical aspects

A number of issues relating to the technical aspects of communication links need to be considered and resolved prior to an incident:

- Ensure that the agencies involved are identified as essential telephone users by the emergency services.

- Identify rooms with multiple computer and telephone points, and establish how easily these can be assigned direct-dial numbers. Decide whether to assign a specific phone number to specific agencies, and how to maintain security of these numbers.

- Determine the location of a helpline, the choice of a telephone number for it and how readily available this number will be.

- Draw up a policy on the use of mobile telephones, choosing between analogue or digital.

- Arrange access to radio communications – your own or via an allied agency.

- Maintain an up-to-date contact list with out-of-hours contact details for:
    - emergency service contacts
    - local hospital/primary care contacts
    - local authority contacts
    - health authority personnel, chief executive, press liaison officers

---

[1] M. Parker and D. Baldwin (1994) 'Warning the public in an emergency', *Civil Protection*; **33**: p10.

[2] Useful advice can be found in: United Kingdom Departments of Health (1993) *Recommendations of the Expert Advisory Group on AIDS. AIDS/HIV-Infected Health Care Workers: Practical Guidance on Notifying Patients*, London: DoH, pp 11–15, and C. Stark, P. Christie and C. Marr (1994), 'Run an emergency helpline', *British Medical Jounrnal*, **309**, pp 44–5.

[3] J. Dakin (1994) 'A media plan is a must', *Civil Protection*, **31**, pp 12–13.

8 Hazard Profiling

In order to plan for major incidents health authorities need to produce a profile of their own area, as well as identifying installations in neighbouring health authority areas which also present a potential hazard due to their size or proximity to the district. Establishing communications with neighbouring health authorities may also be prudent.

Within the health authority

Population

Establish the age and gender profile of the district's population and which are the major population centres.

Socio-economic description

Identify the economic basis of the district – industrial, agricultural or mixed.

Geography

This includes:

- water courses within the district – sources and run-off. Water authorities should be able to advise if any water courses are used for domestic water provision
- low-lying areas or valleys where a toxic plume may persist for a prolonged period
- location of new, current and disused industrial installations and their relationship to population centres, health care facilities, schools, leisure centres and transport. Access to up-to-date maps of the district is vital
- location of recreational centres, local authority evacuation and reception centres, stockpiles of blankets and other resources which may be needed during a major incident.

CIMAH sites

An industrial site which holds, handles or manufactures specified dangerous substances may be classified as a CIMAH site, provided it handles a minimum specified quantity of any substance grouped under a variety of categories in the Control of Industrial Major Accident Hazards Regulations 1984 as amended. Regulations governing CIMAH site classification are complex, and advice should be sought from the local environmental health department or the county/local authority emergency planning officer when seeking to identify all CIMAH sites within the health authority boundary and close to the boundary, if possible. Information of the exact quantities and identity of chemicals used is protected under Section 28 of the CIMAH regulations; there is no reason why the local authority or fire service should not share this information with the health authority under section 28(3)(b). Key information on these sites includes:

- a record of the substances and the quantities of each held as chemicals, intermediates, products and waste materials. Quantities specified in CIMAH plans may not always be accurate

- a record of any antidotes to each substance, and the quantities of each of these held by the site occupational health service
- copies of information provided to those who live near the site

On-site and off-site chemical incident plans will not cover all potential accidents. Copies of these plans may be obtained via the site, the health emergency planning adviser or the county emergency planning officer. It may be worth checking that GPs named in the CIMAH plans have been informed of their involvement. GPs sometimes have no awareness of the plan or their involvement.

Confirm that these plans have been, or are to be, subject to an exercise, and obtain results of exercise debriefings. Consider negotiating to involve the health authority in exercises if it does not already participate.

Nuclear installations

Identifying local nuclear installations should not be difficult. The Nuclear Inspectorate of the Health and Safety Executive licenses nuclear sites under the Nuclear Installations Act 1965. This includes nuclear sites under the control of the Ministry of Defence, which comply with the same regulations. All nuclear installations are subject to the Ionising Radiations Regulations 1985 and are required to have coherent contingency plans to protect the public in the event of a release of radioactivity which must be exercised as part of the licensing requirements. Public health professionals need to be aware that these sites may also operate processes which could present a significant chemical hazard either to the workforce or the public. Nuclear installations also have to provide those living in close proximity to CIMAH sites with similar information. The health authority may wish to ascertain the following:

- information on the radioisotopes which may emanate from the installation in the event of an emergency
- details of any prophylactic agents for any radioisotope including quantities held by the site occupational health service
- copies of information provided to those who live in close proximity to the installation

On-site and off-site nuclear incident response plans will not cover all potential events. Copies of these plans may be obtained via the site, the health emergency planning adviser, or the county emergency planning officer. (It may be worth checking that GPs named in nuclear installation incident plans have been informed – GPs sometimes have no awareness of the plan or their involvement.) Confirm that the plans have been, or are to be, subject to an exercise, and obtain results of exercise debriefings. Consider negotiating to involve the health authority in future exercises if it does not already participate in these.

Non-CIMAH sites

Non-CIMAH sites are more difficult to identify. Useful sources of information include county emergency planning officers, health emergency planning advisers, local authority environmental health officers and local fire services. Information relating to the following may be available:

- gas holding sites
- liquid petroleum sites

- explosive sites
- gas/oil pipelines
- water supplies/reservoirs
- waste outlets/sewage
- location of stations, airports, heliports

In 1994, the Commission of the European Communities published a formal proposal for a new Directive on the Control of Major Accident Hazards (COMAH) involving dangerous substances. The legislation is expected to come into force in 1999.

The scope of premises that will need to be registered under these new regulations will be broader. For instance, exemptions relating to explosives and chemical hazards at nuclear installations will be removed, and a new 'Ecotox' category will be introduced to cover substances which present a hazard to the environment without endangering people directly. The scope of information which must be made publicly available will be expanded.

Local authorities are currently trying to identify potential COMAH sites in their districts, and their records are not yet complete. These systems do not cover small, un-regulated operators. When information about an industry is sought during an incident, the best source may be someone from the site or company itself. Research programmes are being set up to try to document information on COMAH sites.

Contaminated land

Local authorities develop their own strategies for conducting investigations in their area and may subsequently draw up registers based on previous known uses of the land, local knowledge, study of Ordnance Survey maps, historical information, etc. The purpose of this is to identify problem areas of land before redevelopment occurs, to restrict the use of land for certain purposes and to identify the need for remedial action. Once informed, the public health department can monitor any ill effects and look for disease patterns relating to the contaminated land.

Since 1974, records on landfill sites have been kept by the waste regulatory authorities in county councils. Prior to 1974, water authorities had to register landfill sites which might have contaminated water supplies. Some water authorities have transferred their files to local authorities.

In 1988, the Department of the Environment undertook a Derelict Land Survey to which local authorities have access.[1] The survey identified 40,000 hectares of derelict land; these sites are not necessarily contaminated but may merit further investigation.

A database of environmentally hazardous sites has been set up by a private company, Landmark Publications, using many sources of information. The database is aimed at professionals dealing with land – surveyors, lawyers, banks and those who become responsible for environmental risks on land they own.[2]

Mapping systems

A few health and local authorities have been using computerised geographical information systems to assist in their emergency planning and response. It is advisable to contact local health emergency planning advisers or county emergency planning officers to determine whether such systems are available locally.

Identifying hazardous substances

Incidents may also involve chemical agents which are transported throughout the country. The UK is signatory to international agreements covering the carriage of dangerous goods by land, sea or air, requiring hazardous substances to be marked. These markings can assist in the speedy identification of their contents by first responders.

Fire services maintain computer records of hazardous substances and they will respond to enquiries from the NHS. In most emergencies, fire service officers at the scene will establish the type of hazardous substance involved, notify all emergency service representatives and take precautionary measures.

Hazchem

In the UK, a statutory scheme for marking vehicles carrying bulk quantities. i.e. more than 3,000 litres, has been in use since January 1995 (see figure 1). New regulations require UN classification numbers to be given alongside hazard symbols. These are placed next to the Hazchem placard on the body of the tanker.

The Hazchem code gives information under the following headings:

- firefighting methods
- personal protection – level of personal protective clothing to be worn
- risk of violent reaction
- spillage
- evacuation

Figure 1 Vehicle hazard warning panels

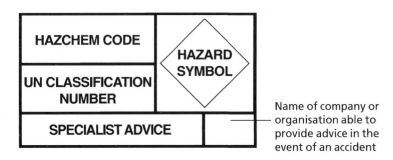

Examples

 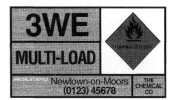

© HMSO 1996

Source: Road Transport Carriage of Dangerous Goods (by Road) Regulations 1996

The code consists of one digit and one or two letters, e.g. 3WE. The digit refers to the firefighting method to be used. The first letter (P, R, S, T, W, X, Y, Z) refers to the spillage action to be taken. A second letter, E, is added for public safety advice. Although evacuation may be necessary, it may be safer for individuals to remain in a building rather than to evacuate.

Copies of the Hazchem code are carried by the emergency services, usually in card form.[3]

The UN classification number is an internationally agreed four-digit code for a specific group of chemicals – e.g. 1789 indicates hydrochloric acid, 3271 refers to ethers, and NOS signifies Not Otherwise Specified.

A contact number for specialist advice in case of emergency is included in the panel. In the UK there is a mutual aid network, CHEMSAFE. The scheme aims to provide advice and assistance to the emergency services. A network of member companies able to attend incidents has been established across the UK. Members of CHEMSAFE also undertake to supply the National Chemical Emergency Centre (NCEC) at Culham, near Didcot, with copies of their Safety Data Sheets. The NCEC is staffed 24 hours a day and can provide information and advice should a chemical company be unidentifiable or unobtainable.

The Chemical Emergency Agency Service (CEAS) is provided on a commercial basis. An annual charge is made to the company based on the number of products being transported. Under this service, companies provide the NCEC with details of products in an agreed format, and are then allowed to display a NCEC telephone number on their vehicle hazard warning panels or package labels. The emergency authorities can obtain the necessary specialised advice for any products by contacting the centre directly.

International operations

Vehicles involved in international operations display a panel divided into two parts. The number at the top of the panel describes the primary hazard of the substance. The number at the bottom is the UN number and identifies the goods carried.

Transport Emergency (TREM) Cards

These are normally carried in the vehicle cab and provide written instructions as required by both international agreement and national legislation for certain commodities. Most of the cards in use in the UK are prepared by the European Chemical Industry Council using a system of standardised phrases and are available in 18 different languages. The information provided on the card is aimed at the driver of the vehicle.

Material Safety Data Sheets

In some countries, Material Safety Data Sheets are required to accompany each product for the benefit of the user. Although not primarily intended for this purpose the information they contain can be used by emergency responders.

International Chemical Safety Card

In the EU, a standard data sheet in 16 sections is required – the International Chemical Safety Card. These cards carry information on the chemical, hazards associated with it, general advice for those exposed to it and environmental data.

Risk assessment of chemical incidents

At the scene

Risk assessment in relation to chemical hazards is a complex and expert process requiring time to consider information and objectively examine a variety of alternative responses. An array of data is required, covering chemical, toxicological, sociological and environmental parameters, and from these a rational assessment is derived. However, the assessment of risks due to a chemical incident often necessitates an immediate evaluation and decisive response – here experience is the best teacher.

In contrast to classical risk assessment, in the case of chemical incidents the response must always tend towards adopting a worst-case assumption. This should only be reconsidered if the response itself may create new hazards or make others worse. As in all rapid response situations information will be scant, and the less information available the more cautious the response should be.

Information should be assessed for reliability, i.e. official data versus public hearsay. It could be potentially disastrous to allocate vital resources to a response only to discover, too late, that the real threat has not been addressed, or has even exacerbated.

Never make vital decisions without taking expert advice from a variety of sources including the emergency services, accident and emergency departments and the health authority's chemical incident adviser. Ensure that all parties are aware of each other's involvement; although one may be the key co-ordinator, decisions should never be based solely upon one agency's opinions.

A rapid risk assessment should always be based upon this framework:

1. **Source** – the agent(s) involved and their physical state
2. **Pathway** – the potential route(s) of exposure
3. **Receptor** – the environmental feature or population at risk

The priority is to evaluate the most threatening and clear linkage between the incident and the public, so there are three countermeasures which should be considered immediately in order to reduce risk:

1. **Source removal** – isolate or disperse it
2. **Pathway removal** – e.g. prevent the volatilisation of spilled liquid or remove contaminated foodstuffs
3. **Receptor removal** – e.g. shelter or evacuate the public

A combination of these strategies may usually be employed. Managerial skill is required to assess the risks, not just of the initial incident but of the mix of countermeasures employed. This will be determined by a number of criteria, including:

• the number and nature of initial casualties

- the possibility of further releases
- the chemical's physical characteristics (volatile, lipophilic, corrosive, flammable, etc.)
- the chemical's toxicity (effects, toxic concentrations etc.)
- the quantity of chemical released to the environment
- the route and fate of the chemical in the environment
- the location of at-risk populations (residential, employees, motorists, etc.)

Information is vital to risk assessment, but decisions should not be delayed excessively if it is scarce. It may be useful to note possible courses of action and rank them. It is important to be as clear as possible about any proposed actions – confusion in a multidisciplinary response can mean wasted time and resources, and may introduce further hazards.

The chemical incident risk assessor should be aware of all available information at the initial response to the incident, and as it develops. If important new information comes to light, the assessment should be adapted accordingly. The risk assessment should always tend towards caution – even more so when the exact constitution of contaminants is in doubt.

Risk assessment may indicate that no further action is required. The reasons for this decision should be recorded.

[1] Department of the Environment (1998) *Survey of Derelict Land in England*, London: HMSO.

[2] Details of the service and charges for searches are available from Landmark IG Ltd, 504 The Chandlery, 50 Westminster Bridge Road, London SE1 7QY.

[3] Home Office and National Chemical Emergency Centre (1997) *Emergency Action Codes and Supplementary Information for Dealing with Incidents Involving Dangerous Substances Conveyed in Bulk by Road or Rail*. Northfleet, Kent: Wilmington Publishing.

9 Toxicology

Toxicology, the science of poisons, defines the internal and external factors which determine and modify the harmful actions of chemical substances, investigates the biological effects of chemicals and assesses health risks.

In response to variations in temperature and pressure, chemical substances may change from one physical form to another. The risks associated with the different physical forms depend on context: an ingot of lead could cause physical injury if dropped on a person, but it might cause serious systemic toxicity if heated and vaporised. Respiratory system damage may be caused by materials in various physical states – solids, liquids, gases, vapours, fumes, mists and aerosols – and systemic absorption will distribute such substances widely throughout the body.

Dose and response

The dose–response relationship is a useful indicator of the toxicity of a chemical. The most toxic substances, such as botulinum toxin, need to be present in body tissue only in trace amounts (i.e. < 5 ng/kg) to exhibit a toxic effect or to prove lethal to humans. In pharmacology the relationship between dose, duration of exposure and toxic effect is well understood. However, much less information is available on many industrial and environmental chemicals.

Toxicokinetics and toxicodynamics

Toxicokinetics is the study of the time course of absorption, distribution, biotransformation and excretion of compounds. Toxicodynamics is the study of the effects of compounds upon the body. These studies assist in evaluating concentrations of toxic chemicals in biological samples from accident victims.

A summary of routes of exposure, absorption, distribution and excretion of toxic chemicals through the human body is given in figure 2. Details of absorption, distribution, metabolism and elimination are not given here, as they are available in textbooks listed in the bibliography.

It is important to bear in mind that individuals exposed to a toxic chemical may absorb it by more than one route, e.g. a gas cloud can lead to inhalation, ingestion, dermal and ocular exposure.

Individual susceptibility

An individual's age, sex, current health, nutritional and hormonal state can all influence their susceptibility to exposure to a particular toxic chemical. Concurrent exposure to other chemicals, and individual genetic variations, e.g. in enzyme activity, should also be considered.

Therefore, assessment of the toxic hazard to an individual requires detailed appraisal of all the factors listed above as well as determining exposure levels, the risk of absorption, whether the absorption will be sufficient to result in a toxic effect, and whether the toxic effect will be immediate or delayed.

Figure 2 Summary of routes of exposure, absorption, distribution and excretion of toxic chemicals in humans

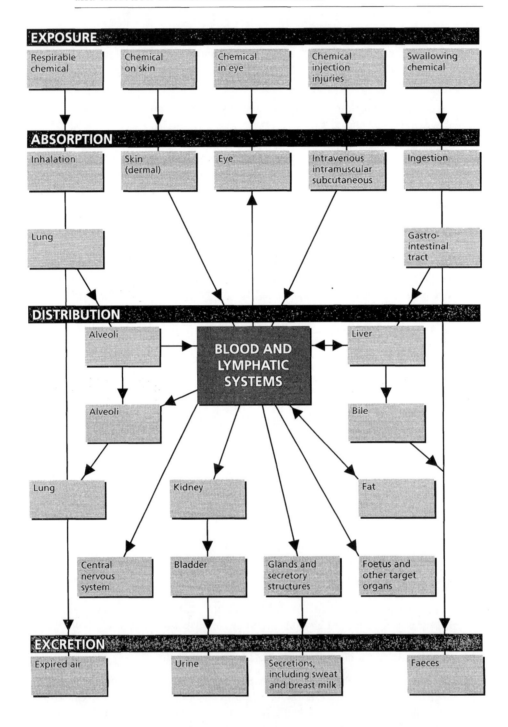

Source: V. Murray (1986) 'Assessment of the Risk of Exposure', in Ward Gardner (ed.) *Substances Hazardous to Health*, Kingston upon Thames; Croner Publications.

Classification of toxic effects

Various methods of classification of toxic effects are available:

- Chemical classification – This is useful in predicting adverse health effects from single substances or groups of similar chemical substances, e.g. heavy metal poisoning, polyaromatic hydrocarbon poisoning.

- Temporal classification – This reflects the response over time to chemical exposure and the resultant toxic effect. Definitions of acute and chronic effects are inevitably arbitrary, but the following are suggested:

  - *acute* effects occur immediately or within 48 hours of exposure, e.g. asphyxia from cyanide, euphoria, hallucinations and coma from inhalation of trichloroethane

  - *chronic* effects occur after a latent period between exposure and outcome, sometimes many years later, e.g. mesothelioma and lung cancer from asbestos, peripheral neuropathy from solvent inhalation or exposure to some pesticides, or may be due to accumulation of chemicals, e.g. lead

- Clinical classification – This encompasses the clinical effects produced by chemicals, such as:

  - *allergenic effects* (e.g. respiratory problems due to formaldehyde)

  - *irritant effects* (e.g. to the eyes, skin, mucous membranes due to chlorine)

  - *carcinogenic effects* (e.g. angiosarcoma of the liver due to vinyl chloride).

- Pathological classification – This is concerned with medical toxicological effects, including those identified by target organ toxicity, such as:

  - *central nervous system* (e.g. anaesthetic and narcotic effects due to hydrocarbons)

  - *peripheral nervous system* (e.g. peripheral neuropathy due to lead)

  - *cardiovascular system* (e.g. an increased incidence of myocardial infarction among viscose rayon workers exposed to carbon disulphide)

  - *renal and hepatic damage* (e.g. carbon tetrachloride and some anaesthetics).

Exposure limits

A number of countries, including the UK, USA and Canada have produced recommended exposure limits for many chemical agents. The majority of these relate to an occupational environment and may be difficult to relate to non-occupational settings. Many of these limits are derived from workforce observational data of variable quality. The health authority's chemical incident adviser may be able to assist in the interpretation of these limits. Two examples of exposure limits are:

- **Occupational Exposure Standard (OES)** – the long-term, day-after-day exposure to an airborne substance. To be considered for OES classification, a substance has to fulfil three specific criteria:

  - The substance can be monitored reasonably accurately at average levels at which there is no indication that it is likely to be injurious to employees if inhaled day after day.

- Exposures to higher concentrations which could reasonably occur in practice are unlikely to produce short- or longer-term effects during the period it takes to identify and correct the cause of excessive exposure.

- The available evidence indicates that compliance with the OES is reasonably practicable.

• **Maximum Exposure Limit (MEL)** – the maximum concentration to which an employee may be exposed under any circumstance, quoted as a time limit ranging from minutes to hours.

Antidotes

The Department of Health document Emergency Planning in the NHS requires district health authorities to assume responsibility for the provision of 'treatment with antidotes or measures to enhance elimination of the toxic chemical from the body'.[1]

There are at least 36 clinically effective antidotes, and clearly it is neither feasible nor cost-effective for stocks of all of them to be held by each health authority. A list of antidotes can be found in Appendix 2. Some districts hold very few, but others have gone so far as to match the antidotes held to the perceived chemical risks in the area. No directives have been issued and no common approach is advised in the literature, which may explain the considerable variation currently throughout the UK regarding which antidotes are available at district level, what quantities are held, what additional stocks exist at regional level, and who knows of their existence.

The distinction between those antidotes which need to be given immediately and those which can be administered within a few hours will have a bearing on which should be held locally and which could be ordered from either a regional or a national centre in the event of need.

In certain industries where highly toxic substances are used, e.g. cyanide in forestry, it is a legal requirement to stock antidotes for immediate use. However, there are no specific HSE guidelines determining the quantities or storage locations of these antidotes in relation to the workforce. It is worth checking with occupational health physicians in your area what antidotes are available and how these could be obtained in an emergency.

Public health physicians might consider discussing with their consultant colleagues in A&E whether an emergency kit of antidotes should be held, where it should be located, and how to ensure its location is well documented.

Hospital pharmacies may be the most appropriate place to keep an emergency antidotes kit, as infrequent use of some of the compounds means that reviewing use-by dates, stocktaking and re-ordering is an essential routine.

Some drugs, such as diazepam for chloroquine toxicity, are routinely available, but **the dosages required as antidotes may differ from the usual regimens**.

Radiation

In the event of a radiation incident early contact with the National Radiological Protection Board is essential.

Exposure to radiation can affect the human body and may come from a variety of sources. The three main types are:

- **Alpha particles** – this danger arises from the accidental inhalation or ingestion of particles which remain in the body causing continuing irradiation to the surrounding tissues. Because the particles are only weakly penetrating and the risk of inhalation or ingestion is slight, the patient does not pose a risk to the staff who provide appropriate care. These patients would be passed to the medical teams directly as they do not require decontamination, but would be assessed later by the radiation protection adviser. Patients who are exposed to alpha particles may, however, require decontamination if they have additionally become contaminated with other particles.

- **Beta particles** – can penetrate the skin and cause burns, but again the main risk is to the contaminated casualty, who may ingest or inhale the particles, causing tissue damage.

- **Gamma radiation** – is emitted like radio waves or x-rays and will pass through the body causing cell damage. The effect is governed by the distance from the source and the length of exposure. The risk of irradiaton with gamma radiation is reduced by:
  - limiting the exposure period
  - shielding the body with dense materials
  - keeping the source as far away as possible from the patient and rescuers

  This type of radiation can be measured with radiometers, and the level of exposure assessed and monitored when exposure occurs, but after the event the assessment is clinical.

---

[1] National Health Service Management Executive (1990) *Emergency Planning in the NHS: Health Service Arrangements for Dealing with Major Incidents*, HC(90)25, London: NHSME. Includes 'Handbook of Emergency Planning Guidance' (London: DoH). See also National Health Service Management Executive (1993) *Arrangements for Dealing with Health Aspects of Chemical Contamination Incidents*, HSG(93)38, Leeds: NHSME.

10 Exposure assessment

Important elements of any exposure assessment are identification of the agent(s) involved, individual patient health status and toxicological assessments, and an assessment of wider environmental contamination which may have implications for human health, such as land contamination and the potential to contaminate water supplies and foodstuffs.

It is important to undertake a full clinical assessment including baseline physiological, haematological and biochemical assessments, in order to:

- determine the nature and severity of any health effects allegedly associated with exposure to a toxic substance
- provide comparative data for the future monitoring of an individual's health
- provide evidence for legal reasons, e.g. forensic evidence

It is important to take toxicological samples in order to:

- check whether individuals have been exposed to any toxic substance(s)
- identify the supposed substance(s)
- gauge whether an individual has been exposed to a toxic dose
- provide a baseline measurement by which to monitor excretion and elimination of the substance
- provide evidence for legal reasons, e.g. forensic evidence

It is important to take environmental samples in order to:

- check whether an environment has been contaminated by any toxic substance(s)
- identify the supposed substance(s)
- assess whether contamination poses a health risk to residents or others
- assess potential secondary effects, e.g. food contamination
- plan decontamination measures
- provide evidence for legal reasons, e.g. prosecution, forensic evidence

Identifying the agents

During the initial stages of a chemical incident, efforts are directed towards identifying the chemical substances involved and providing the appropriate supportive care. A variety of sources may be used (see Chapter 8).

Clinical assessment

Medical examination

The clinical assessment of any patient who claims to have been exposed to a chemical agent should be carefully documented as this will form the contemporaneous and baseline record for future follow-up and legal purposes. A careful history should be obtained. This should include:

- when the exposure occurred
- duration of exposure
- where the person was at the time of exposure
- the symptoms the person claims to have suffered

An examination of the person should be undertaken, noting both positive and negative signs.

Routine physiological, haematological and biochemical investigations should be undertaken, including:

• respiratory function tests

• routine haematology and biochemistry tests

• radiological investigations

Toxicological sampling

DoH guidance states that health authorities should anticipate the need to collect toxicological samples in order to assess health effects both in the acute phase and for short-term and long-term surveillance.

The cost of assaying samples may have to be borne ultimately by the health authority. Even though obtaining funding approval may delay analysis, **there is no reason to delay taking samples**. It is better to take and store samples which may be discarded later than to miss the opportunity to take early samples which may provide evidence of the highest blood levels of the toxic substance. One option is to perform assays on one or two sentinel cases and then decide whether to test the remainder.

Seek expert advice from the health authority's chemical incident adviser or local provider of chemical pathology services on whether a particular toxicological assay exists, which laboratories, including public analyst laboratories, can perform the analysis, the cost per assay (there may be discounts for bulk testing) and any special precautions necessary when sampling. Health authorities should contact these laboratories for estimates of cost and specific sampling instructions (laboratory contact details are given in Appendix 1).

The health authority has a pivotal role in identifying exposed individuals, ensuring samples are obtained via hospitals, community health facilities, general practice surgeries or alternative locations, if appropriate, and ensuring consistency in sample-taking procedures.

Environmental sampling of suspect material

Public health physicians should discuss any proposed sampling of the environment with environmental health officers and the health authority chemical incident adviser. Important questions for the formulation of public health advice are likely to arise from the test results, including measures to treat exposed individuals and measures to minimise further exposure to the chemicals.

Sampling of chemicals in the environment may be undertaken by a number of agencies, including local authority environmental health departments. Before undertaking any sampling, environmental health officers are likely to give careful consideration to the reasons for sampling, as this will assist in determining the level of resources needed, but sampling is usually undertaken to determine a level of exposure to either persons or the environment following the release of a chemical substance.

It is worth remembering that taking swabs from firefighter's garments may help in discovering the possibly unknown chemicals involved.

Blind screen

If there will be some delay in obtaining expert advice, or if the substance involved is unknown it may be worth considering taking a small range of specimens to provide enough scope for a toxicology blind screen.

- **Use sterile water, or dry cotton wool if the skin is reasonably clean, to pre-clean the venepuncture site** – proprietary wipes or swabs, e.g. Mediswabs, contain solvents and trace chemicals which could interfere with assays.

- **Use blood bottles with plastic or lined metal tops** – chemicals can leach from blood tubes with gel separators or those which contain mucous heparin solutions, vacutainers, soft-plastic bottles, reusable containers and rubber bungs, contaminating the specimens.

- **Store all samples at 4°C, and send them for sampling within 48 hours** – otherwise trace elements such as mercury will leach into the sample bottle.

- Pack each sample separately – to avoid damage in transit.

In order of importance, the blind screen should consist of:

- **Adults**
  - 10 ml blood in a plastic lithium heparin tube
  - 5 ml blood in a glass lithium heparin tube
  - 4 ml blood in an EDTA tube
  - 50 ml urine without preservative
- **Children**
  - 5 ml blood in a glass lithium heparin tube
  - 5 ml blood in an EDTA tube
  - 50 ml urine without preservative

If the following substances are suspected, take the following samples:

- **Metal/trace element**
  - 4 ml blood in an EDTA tube
  - 50 ml urine without preservative
- **Pesticide/herbicide**
  - 5 ml blood in a lithium heparin tube
  - 50 ml urine without preservative
- **Rodenticide**
  - 5 ml clotted blood only
- **Solvent**
  - 2 ml blood in a lithium heparin tube, preferably glass, with minimal air space

Biological assays are also available for drugs, cyanide, alcohols and glycol esters. Even if the suspected toxins are not listed in the services provided by an individual laboratory, special analyses can sometimes be developed if the need arises. Always collect samples, and discuss the matter with the National Poisons Information Service as soon as possible.

The sampling kit should consist of:

1 x 5 ml glass tube for clotted blood

1 x 10 ml plastic lithium heparin tube

1 x 4 ml EDTA tube

1 x 60 ml universal container for urine

1 x form

1 x plastic container for form

1 x container for the whole kit[1]

[1] Kits for blind screening are available from the Medical Toxicology Unit, Avonlea Road, London SE14 5ER.

11 Decontamination

Precautions

One important similarity between chemical and communicable disease incidents is the risk of cross-contamination from affected individuals to health care workers. The adoption of universal precautions which apply to good infection control practice will help obviate this risk to staff dealing with patients during a chemical incident.

Other routes of potential cross-contamination should be considered. For example if a car has been driven through a chemical plume, the car engine may need to be washed down before re-starting, to prevent wider dispersal of the chemical.

When hosing down people, animals, land, vehicles or equipment is being considered, it is important to ensure, where possible, that run-off water is collected to enable safe disposal or analysis. Communication links with local water utilities will be necessary to obtain advice about run-off of contaminated water entering sewage systems during an emergency situation.

Decontamination at the incident scene

Where practicable the emergency services should decontaminate patients before they are transported to an accident and emergency centre. Often a cordon will be put in place by the emergency services, limiting access to and egress from the contaminated areas by means of exclusion, contamination-reduction and support zones.

The fire service use a portable decontamination system devised to decontaminate their own officers. This can also be used for other emergency services and, where possible, for members of the public. Various types exist.

One consists of a tubular-framed shower delivering 1,125 litres of water a minute at 5 bars pressure. This is adequate to deal with most water-miscible chemicals and achieves decontamination in about two minutes. The disadvantages are that the water is usually cold and the fine droplets generated increase the risk of inhalation of the substance. This system is therefore best suited to firefighters wearing breathing apparatus.

It is the responsibility of the fire service to provide a holding tank for contaminated water. The health authority should check the availability of such a tank before rather than during an incident.

The ambulance service should generally try to remove as much contaminated clothing from patients as possible before they board the ambulance; the clothing should be left at the site. There is a recognised need to have 'dirty' and 'clean' ambulance sites where possible. Ambulance staff may be reluctant to transport casualties unless they have been decontaminated.

As a precautionary measure the ambulance may be lined with plastic sheeting and the windows left open. Near crashes have resulted when ambulance crews have experienced adverse effects from volatile substances which have contaminated the ambulance interior, while transporting contaminated casualties.

A contaminated ambulance should only be used to transport other contaminated casualties from the same incident. It may be necessary for the ambulance and equipment to be decontaminated or decommissioned. In a life-threatening emergency where no other vehicles are available it may be acceptable to use a contaminated ambulance to convey uncontaminated casualties provided precautions such as plastic sheeting are used.

It may be necessary to arrange for exposed individuals to be decontaminated away from the incident scene but prior to arrival at hospital. The health authority may need to liaise with local authority colleagues to identify potential decontamination centres. Schools and leisure centres may have the capacity to provide showering facilities to large numbers of people, so they may be most suitable.

Decontamination at the hospital

Health authority plans should include the provision of adequate decontamination facilities, as set out in HBN 22 1988.[1] Some recently built hospitals include purpose-built decontamination rooms, whereas others have had to adapt pre-existing facilities. One of the commonest problems appears to be that the designated decontamination room has been decommissioned to be used as a storage space or office which would need to be emptied in the event of an emergency. (Health Building standards for decontamination facilities can be found in appendix 7.)

[1] Department of Health and Social Services (1988) *Health Building Note 22: Accident and Emergency Department*, HBN 22 1988, London: DHSS.

12 Public safety – shelter versus evacuation

Background

In the event of a chemical incident where the public may be exposed to a toxic vapour cloud and/or the risk of fire and explosion, two options for protective action exist – sheltering or evacuation.

At present, a consultant in communicable disease control or consultant in public health medicine may only rarely be involved in the decision-making process. The decision on what, if any, action should be taken in an acute incident usually rests with the police, taking into account advice received from the fire, ambulance and social services. As part of a developing integrated approach to all incidents, the consultant in communicable disease control/consultant in public health medicine should be a member of any response team, as this means that emergency services, ambulance control and A&E departments will be more likely to involve them.

The police tend to view the ambulance service as the main health service representatives in any emergency planning forum, so the health authority and its public health department are often not considered to have a role as advisers or decision-makers during an incident. To participate actively in this process, the health authority may need to contact the police to request that its nominated representative be included in the network of those notified during an incident.

If the health authority is called upon to give an opinion from the public health population-based perspective, some familiarity with the issues involved will be useful. Any pre-existing local guidance/information should be obtained, in advance, from any CIMAH site or nuclear installation off-site plan.

CIMAH sites

Under Schedule 8 of the Control of Industrial Major Accident Hazards Regulations 1990, CIMAH site operators must supply safety information to members of the public resident in a zone liable to be affected in a major accident. The size of the zone concerned is established between HSE consultants and the operators, and is typically an area within a 2 – 3 kilometre radius of the site.

Local households are supplied with an information card outlining:

- the basic site activity
- a description of the hazardous substances stored
- description of the emergency warning signal, e.g. activation of a siren with details of siren tests
- emergency action to take, e.g. effective sheltering advice, tuning in to radio frequencies for further instructions, etc.

The public near a CIMAH site need to be issued with these instructions for immediate action because it is likely there will be little time to give out information during the early stages of an incident. Even with low windspeeds of 2 m/s, the front of a gas cloud may have travelled 1.2 kilometres in 10 minutes, leaving the emergency services with insufficient time for pre-emptive action. The health authority should obtain a copy of this advice, which may prove helpful during an incident.

Radiological incidents

The need for evacuation in the event of the release or threatened release of radioactive material is addressed in Arrangements for Responding to Nuclear Emergencies.[1] Advice should be sought from experts at the Health and Safety Executive and the National Radiological Protection Board. A sample data collection form for people attending a reception centre can be found in Appendix 5.

Other information sources

Geographical information systems may assist in mapping the potential spread of a toxic plume. Also, CHEMET, part of the Meteorological Office at Bracknell, can be consulted by the police by local agreement when there is an incident. An assessment of local weather conditions is made, and a fax is sent showing the probable drift of a plume.

Sheltering or evacuation – the pros and cons

Sheltering

A considerable degree of protection is afforded by sheltering in a house. Buildings dampen fluctuations in atmospheric turbulence, reducing infiltration by gases. Even in a poorly sealed house infiltration may be reduced by a factor of 10; when windows and doors are sealed, this increases to a factor of 30 – 50.

Effective sheltering entails:

* closing doors and windows
* minimising draughts by sealing windows and doors with paper/tape or damp towels
* turning off central heating
* turning off mechanical ventilation
* going to an upper floor, if possible to an interior room where ventilation is less
* avoiding bathrooms and kitchens, which tend to have higher ventilation rates
* keeping pets indoors
* breathing through a wet cloth over the face if the atmosphere becomes uncomfortable
* having access to a radio to tune into the local radio station for further information and advice

The public also need to be advised not to use the telephone unless absolutely vital, to prevent unnecessary jamming of lines. They may be asked to notify neighbours who may not have heard the warning.

Communications systems must be in place to ensure that people go outside to the fresh air as soon as the hazard has passed. If inhabitants remain sheltered too long they could end up being exposed to a higher cumulative dose than they would have received outside. Some people may be severely incapacitated and will need to be assisted from their homes. Prompt medical attention is required to screen for those at risk from the potential effects of exposure to irritant gases, e.g. for pulmonary oedema which may occur after a latent period of 12–24 hours.

Evacuation

Evacuation is a measure of last resort when the public would be in serious danger if they stayed. Specific instances would be:

- **Before an incident (precautionary)**
    - risk of imminent explosion
    - small leak likely to escalate sharply
    - release/ threatened release of radioactive materials
- **During an incident**
    - spread of fire or continuation of a hazardous release over a prolonged period
- **After an incident**
    - gross environmental contamination

Evacuation is not appropriate in a short-term toxic cloud situation. It is feasible only if it can be confidently predicted that there is sufficient time to evacuate people before the incident escalates.

The time available to effect evacuation will depend on:

- the time required to make the decision to evacuate – the emergency services' response time
- the time required to communicate with the public – depending on method chosen, e.g. door-to-door, via loudhailers, radio/TV networks, any language barriers, whether translators are needed
- the time of day – it is more difficult to warn people effectively at 4 a.m. than 8 p.m.
- the time necessary for the public to prepare to move – to collect clothes, medication, baby supplies, pets, cheque books, credit cards, and to secure their homes
- the time required for the public to move.

The decision to evacuate is also affected by:

- the population profile – numbers of elderly, handicapped and immobile, whether there are any residential/nursing homes in the affected area, the number of people with special needs living in institutions, any people on dialysis machines or others at special risk
- the extent of the road network
- transport availability – public and private (in the UK, 30% of households do not have a car and will need assistance)
- blockage of roadways – e.g. flooding, snow
- hazardous travel conditions – e.g. fog, sleet, ice, snow
- consideration of the effect on evacuees of:
    - outside temperature
    - psychological trauma/medical risks

  − risk of damage and looting to property

  − cost

• how large a zone should be evacuated

• the health risk to the police cordon

Checklist of questions

1. Is the substance harmful to the public?

  − highly toxic/toxic/irritant/non-irritant

  − short-term/long-term effects

  − explosive/non-explosive

2. Will the public be exposed?

  − substance contained

  − potential for release

  − capable of dispersal via wind, rain, etc.

  − public in path of projected dispersal route

  − distance, height of plume, meteorological conditions, stability of weather conditions

3. Will dilution factors minimise the risk?

4. When will the public be exposed (time of day)?

  − already exposed

  − imminently

  − not for a few hours

5. How long will the exposure last?

  − few minutes

  − hours

  − days

¹ Health and Safety Executive (1994) *Arrangements for Responding to Nuclear Emergencies*, London: HMSO.

13 Counselling

Stress reactions

Incidents involving the release of potentially toxic chemicals are viewed as sinister events. Experience has shown that a significant increase in stress-related psychiatric and psychosomatic symptoms can occur, even several years later, when there has been an environmental threat. Parson's work indicated that the public's perception of the environment and potential pollutants is almost more important in its effect on health than the pollutant itself.[1]

Factors influencing stress reactions include:

- uncertainty about the nature, extent and future health implications of the accident – for oneself as well as family and friends
- displacement due to housing and job insecurity, contamination of homes, reduction in orders for local products
- economic insecurity, fears about compensation, insurance claims
- social rejection of those considered to be contaminated
- cultural pressure related to conflicting public opinion about how people should behave
- hostility towards and mistrust of industry, doctors, politicians
- guilt, if working in an industry that caused the problem

Features of stress reactions include:

- mood disorders – emotional 'stunning' in the acute phase, giving rise to depressed or anxious mood
- cognitive disturbance
- intrusive thoughts

However, only a few go on to develop a modified form of post-traumatic stress disorder.

Groups most likely to have adverse reactions include:

- those with the greatest amount of personal involvement including rescue workers and direct helpers
- parents of young children
- those with a pre-existing history of mental illness

One of the most crucial elements in reducing psychological morbidity is to provide the public with adequate, credible information in a structured way.

Informing the public

It is vital to start providing information as soon as possible. Fassenden-Rader described how the events surrounding an incident are a valuable indicator of later acceptance of information, where, 'in communities where residents themselves first experienced a problem and later called it to the attention of officials, the risk information subsequently given to them was perceived as an understatement of the real dangers or even as a whitewash'.[2]

Provision of counselling

Health authority plans should include arrangements for the provision of counselling both for rescue workers and the public.

Counselling the public

Members of the public often benefit from the opportunity to ventilate their immediate fears, talking over what has happened, what might happen and what needs to be done. Those at risk are likely to live in a concentric distribution around the incident site, although the limits may be difficult to define.

Some will recover after one session of counselling, some will need much more. People are often invited to come forward, but this is an obvious instance of self-selection. Public health physicians should seek to identify particularly vulnerable groups with the assistance of support and voluntary services.

Perception of risk

In 1991, Stoffle et al. described the concept of a 'risk perception shadow' – the geocultural area which perceives itself to be at risk.[3] Local perception of risk may cover a greater geographical area than that identified by the authorities. People outside the designated risk area may receive no information nor be invited to a health screening, and consequently may feel largely ignored. It may be worth widening the area an extra few kilometres in order to counter this.

Who should do the counselling?

It is important to distinguish between advice, information and counselling.[4] Clinical psychologists and professional counsellors (the social services department may have a list) are the most appropriate professionals to give the counselling. However, other organisations such as the British Association for Counselling may help with identifying counsellors to whom individuals may be referred, while bodies such as the Samaritans and Relate (the latter specifically in the context of couple counselling) may be able to provide additional support.

Most people's health fears diminish over time. The counsellor must therefore try to distinguish between those people who require more prolonged follow-up and those in need of referral for psychiatric support.

The following findings from the Braer disaster, where 85,000 tonnes of crude oil were discharged from the tanker MV Braer into the sea at Garth's Ness off Shetland in January 1993, may be illuminating:

- Initially, 58% of people perceived a health risk from the spill. This later reduced to 21%.
- Inhalation of the oil was perceived to be the biggest risk, especially since inhalation was related to symptoms that were easily recalled; 21% also identified indirect effects such as worry and anxiety as contributing to health risk.
- The events surrounding an incident are a valuable indicator of later acceptance of information.

Important lessons

The effects on health of people's perceptions about the environment and the potential pollutants are almost more important than the potential pollutant itself.

Risk perception shadow mapping enables the provision of counselling services to be targeted. Be aware that the area initially designated may have to be enlarged.

[1] R. Parsons 1991 'Potential influences of environmental perception on human health', *Journal of Environmental Psychology* 1991; 11: 1–23.

[2] J. Fassenden-Rader, J. Fitchen and J.S. Heath 'Providing risk information in communities: factors influencing what is heard and accepted', *Science, Technology & Human Values* 12: 3 & 4, pp.94–101.

[3] R.W. Stoffle, M.W. Traugott, J.V. Stone, P.D. McIntyre, F.V. Jensen, R.C. Davidson (1991). 'Risk perception mapping: using ethnography to define the locally affected population for a low-level radioactive waste storage facility in Michigan, USA', *American Anthropology* 93(3), pp. 611–35.

[4] A good source for counselling procedures is: United Kingdom Department of Health (1993) *Recommendations of the Expert Advisory Group on AIDS. AIDS/HIV – Infected Health Care Workers: Practical guidance on notifying patients,* London: 1994; DoH.

14 Epidemiological approaches

Data collection

One of the most important aspects of any epidemiological investigation of a chemical or other incident is the quality of data. To maximise the quality of data collection, where possible information-gathering should be carried out in a structured manner. The use of a variety of previously prepared data collection forms, some of which can be modified to suit the circumstances of an incident, should prove useful.

Literature review

Access to medical and possibly toxicological databases is important. This will allow a rapid search of the medical literature for information on the agent(s) implicated in an incident. The health authority's chemical incident adviser is also likely to be able to conduct a search of toxicological databases for information to support public health advice. The Chemical Incident Management Handbook (part of this series) will provide information on a range of the more common agents in a standardised format.

Descriptive epidemiology

This should provide a basic picture of the situation – time, place and person. Data should accurately describe the time frame of the incident as it develops and when it ends, the area affected, including any population centres, and the numbers of people exposed, presumed exposed, affected (symptomatic/clinically confirmed) and deceased.

Analytical epidemiology

This is likely to be a later exercise, probably after the acute incident is over. One important aspect of this form of epidemiological exercise will be the formulation of a case definition for individuals exposed to a particular chemical agent. This should be made in consultation with others, including those treating patients and the health authority's chemical incident adviser.

A decision on the type of study to be undertaken will also have to be made. It is advisable to consult colleagues in academic epidemiology or public health medicine departments with a special interest in environmental epidemiology or expertise in small-area statistics.

In addition to the standard cohort and case-control studies, it may be possible to undertake dose–response investigations. An important prerequisite for such a study will be the availability of information on the dose experienced by individuals exposed to particular agents.

Cluster investigations[1]

A cluster has been defined by Knox as 'a geographically bounded group of occurrences of sufficient size and concentration to be unlikely to have occurred by chance.'[2]

The investigation of a perceived cluster of adverse health effects is not an isolated epidemiological or statistical exercise. An appropriate response by public health authorities requires a recognition of the complexity of such investigations, in addition to the possession and application of specific skills, including an awareness of the social and cultural issues of the situation, understanding of risk perception, knowledge of the functions of the media, and awareness of the potential legal ramifications of the investigation.

Managing perceived clusters is a type of surveillance encompassing the ongoing collection, analysis, and dissemination of information important to the public health response. The primary aim of the approach is not aetiological investigation (public health practitioners should note that any method employed is unlikely to identify an aetiological association). The aim should be to determine whether a cluster in time, space, or both exists – hence the emphasis on examining patterns in time, space, or both. Investigators should be aware of the different ways in which people respond to stressful situations and react to uncertainties. It is likely the investigator will have to be able to address the public perception of a problem responsibly and sympathetically, even when there is no demonstrable underlying community health problem or cluster of disease.

The public health physician has a duty to communicate the degree of risk inherent in a situation under study to the community in an easily understood form – the presentation of numbers is unlikely to prove sufficient. The population's perception of risk may not match mathematical or scientific assessments, and putting a risk into perspective with commonly experienced risks may prove helpful. Care should be taken to do this in a sensitive, non-condescending manner. Public health physicians should be aware of media imperatives – the factors which influence the choice and presentation of stories by different sections of the media including the pictorial/visual appeal, the presence of conflict or controversy, a strong emotive content, and a target for attributing blame. There may also be legal ramifications to any investigation, making it essential for public health departments to have a system for keeping accurate records of investigations.

Guidelines for approach

This describes one system for managing clusters. It may prove appropriate to end an investigation at any of the points in this process. (Procedures and responses for each point in the system can be found in Section Three.)

Initial contact

This is an opportunity to collect information from person(s) reporting perceived health events and to communicate the complex nature of clusters to the informant(s).

The health authority should have a system for handling such inquiries. This should include identifying the department within the health authority responsible for managing cluster queries, a means of initial data collection, general information to be offered to callers, a method for obtaining further information on cases, routine recording for each query, informing the press officer or equivalent within the health authority, and producing a written response to callers.

If a decision to proceed to further investigation is taken, there needs to be a method for evaluating whether an excess of health events has occurred.

Preliminary evaluation

Data from the contact and other sources are used to perform an assessment of observed versus expected occurrences of implicated health events. This should provide a quick, rough estimate of likelihood that an important health event has occurred. Following this, a decision to conduct further investigation into specific cases may be taken.

Case evaluation

Case-specific data are obtained and reviewed to verify the diagnosis for each implicated health event. This will assist in the formation of a case definition for further investigation. This process can be time-consuming and costly.

Occurrence evaluation

This process should define the characteristics of the cluster. A study protocol should be produced, including a detailed literature review and an outline of data sources, collection methods and analyses to be employed. The objectives of the study should be to determine whether an excess of adverse health events has occurred and to describe the epidemiological characteristics of the situation.

Major feasibility study

This should determine whether it is possible to conduct an epidemiological study linking the implicated health events and a putative exposure. The health authority is likely to require assistance from an epidemiological unit specialising in such investigations. If such a study proves possible, a decision should be made whether to proceed to a formal aetiological investigation.

Aetiological investigations

This study is likely to investigate any epidemiological and public health questions raised by the initial cluster investigation. It will take the form of a standard epidemiological investigation of potential disease–exposure relationships, and may not specifically investigate the initial cluster.

Statistical and epidemiological techniques

A variety of methods is employed during the investigation of suspected clusters. There is no single technique which will prove appropriate for all situations. It is important that anyone investigating a suspect cluster seeks expert advice on which technique is best suited to the given circumstances including a discussion of its strengths and weaknesses. A number of computer software packages have been produced and others are being developed to assist in the statistical analysis of cluster investigation (these include an IBM PC program, CLUSTER, which has been developed by CDC, Atlanta). There is an ongoing debate within the international scientific community regarding the robustness of the inferences and assumptions made by programmers.

[1] Much of this information is a précis of Centres for Disease Control and Prevention (1990) 'Guidelines for investigating clusters of health events.' *Morbidity and Mortality Weekly Report*, **39:** (RR-11) pp. 1–23.

[2] E.G. Knox (1989) 'Detection of clusters', in P. Elliott (ed.) *Methodology of Enquiries into Disease Clustering*, London: Small Area Health Statistics Unit, pp.17–20.

15 Legislation relating to chemical incidents

The legislation relating to chemical incidents is both wide and varied. There is no single authority within the UK responsible for dealing with major emergencies such as a chemical incident. Accordingly, there is no single piece of legislation applicable to such circumstances. However, each of the principal agencies that is likely to be involved is either responsible for enforcing legislation or is an authority with a legal basis.

There is no legal requirement for the costs of dealing with an incident to be paid by the party responsible, such as the owner of a factory, tanker, etc., although in many instances the instigator of the incident will carry public liability insurance to enable them to contribute towards the costs. If any damage or injury arises, civil proceedings may be taken to obtain compensation. A detailed explanation of civil action procedures is beyond the scope of this book, but it must be borne in mind that there is always the chance that any civil action taken by a third party may require evidence from the public health physician responsible for the area in which an incident arises.

The purpose of including a brief description of the major legislation in this book is to give the reader an overview of the legal responsibilities of those who use, store and transport chemicals and hazardous materials; the precise interpretation of the law is a matter for the appropriate enforcing authority, their legal advisers and the judiciary. The summary of legislation below is not comprehensive, nor does it detail all the potential offences under each piece of legislation. In particular, it does not address the criminal legislation that may be enforced by the police, and the relevant local authority planning and emergency planning legislation.

Industrial sites

Control of Industrial Major Accident Hazards Regulations 1984 (as amended)

Known by the acronym CIMAH, the principal objective of these regulations is to prevent major accidents at certain specified industrial installations affecting people and the nearby environment, and to limit the effects of any which do occur. These regulations require the preparation of on-site emergency plans, and that the relevant local authority prepare off-site plans. The HSE is the enforcing authority. These regulations implement the Seveso Directive.

Control of Major Accident Hazards (COMAH)

This is a new EC directive intended to improve the control of major hazards and is expected to come into force in 1999. It will require additional sites, not covered at present by CIMAH, to produce emergency plans, and site operators to place increased emphasis on managerial and organisational issues by instituting a major accident prevention policy. In addition, local authorities will be required to test these emergency plans at regular intervals.

Notification of Installations Handling Hazardous Substances Regulations 1982

These regulations require operators of sites where certain specified quantities and types of materials are stored or handled to notify details to the HSE.

Health and Safety at Work Act 1974

This is the principal enabling Act concerning all aspects of health and safety at work. The responsibilities for enforcement are divided between the HSE and local authorities, although the HSE has the major responsibility for industrial sites and for the transport of chemicals.

Chemicals (Hazard Information and Packaging) Regulations 1994

Known by the acronym CHIP, the aim of these regulations is to protect people and the environment from the detrimental effect of chemicals by means of labelling and the provision of safety data sheets. The regulations also require chemical suppliers to assess whether the chemicals are dangerous or not, using the classification system detailed in the schedules.

Control of Substances Hazardous to Health Regulations 1994

Known by the acronym COSHH, these regulations replaced the original 1988 regulations and apply to toxic, harmful, corrosive or irritant substances defined in the CHIP regulations and to all places of work. The COSHH regulations require an assessment of risk to employees arising from work, and the steps necessary to control the risk. Maximum exposure limits are defined in Schedule 1 of the regulations.

Dangerous Substance (Notification and Marking of Sites) Regulations 1990

The aim of these regulations is to ensure that the health and safety enforcement authorities and fire service have information about certain sites where dangerous substances are stored or used.

Nuclear installations

Radioactive Substances Act 1993

This Act requires the registration of sites which store radioactive substances and the licensing of discharges to air, water and disposal of solid wastes. The Act is enforced by the Environment Agency.

Ionising Radiation Regulations 1985

These regulations implement EC Directive 80/836, as amended, and were made under the Health and Safety at Work Act 1974. Their aim is to protect workers and the general public against ionising radiation when it is used in the workplace, by requiring notification to the HSE of sites where ionising radiation is used, restricting exposure to as low as is reasonably practicable, and ensuring that doses of ionising radiation received do not exceed specified dose limits. An approved code of practice has been issued by the Health and Safety Commission.

Food and drinking water contamination

Food Safety Act 1990

This Act gives local authorities powers to deal with the safety of food during preparation and sale.

The Food Safety (General Food Hygiene) Regulations 1995

These regulations require that food handling operations be carried out hygienically and safely. These are also enforced by local authority environmental health staff.

Food and Environment Protection Act 1985

Known by the acronym FEPA, Part 1 of this Act permits emergency orders to be made where there are major contamination risks to food production in agriculture or elsewhere from the release of toxic chemicals and substances. These orders are made by the Secretary of State for the Environment and/or the Minister of Agriculture.

Water Supply (Water Quality) Regulations 1989 (as amended)

These regulations incorporate standards to ensure that drinking water is wholesome. The Drinking Water Inspectorate (part of the Department of Environment) monitors compliance and also investigates incidents affecting water quality.

Private Water Supplies Regulations 1991 in England and Wales

These require local authorities to monitor and ensure compliance with similar standards.

Environmental pollution

Environmental Protection Act 1990

Known by the acronym EPA, Part I of this Act requires the authorisation of certain industrial processes.

Part III includes specific sections which permit actions by local authorities and individuals to deal with statutory nuisances, including smoke, fumes or gases from private dwellings, dust, steam, smell or other effluvia from industrial or trade premises, and accumulation or deposit of materials.

The Environmental Protection (Prescribed Processes and Substances) Regulations 1991 (as amended)

These classify processes into Parts A and B. Part A processes are the most complex and polluting; these fall under integrated pollution control (IPC) and are enforced by the Environment Agency in England and Wales, and the Scottish Environmental Protection Agency in Scotland. It requires that the 'best practicable environmental option' be considered in relation to pollution of more than one environmental medium, i.e. atmosphere, hydrosphere, geosphere to ensure that the pollution as a whole is reduced. Part B processes concern emissions to the atmosphere only. Specific conditions are applied by the regulators to limit pollution. Local authority environmental health staff are responsible for Part B in England and Wales.

Clean Air Act 1993

This has specific sections that permit local authorities to take legal action in relation to 'dark smoke' from industrial and trade premises.

Water Resources Act 1991 and Water Industries Act 1991

These Acts replace the Water Act 1989, and enable the Environment Agency or Scottish Environmental Protection Agency to deal with water pollution and water resource management. It should be noted that these authorities' responsibilities relate to water pollution arising in public sewers as well as in rivers and other watercourses.

Transport of hazardous substances

Road Transport (Carriage of Dangerous Goods by Road) Regulations 1996

These deal with the transport of dangerous goods, other than radioactive materials and explosives, by imposing prohibitions on, and requirements for, the carriage of dangerous goods by road in any container, tank or vehicle. They include the requirement to display specified information, including information at the rear of the vehicle (see chapter 8). These regulations are enforced by the HSE.

Dangerous Substances in Harbour Areas Regulations 1987

These are similar to the CIMAH regulations, requiring notification before bringing dangerous substances into port and harbour areas. The regulations also require the preparation of emergency plans, if not already made under the CIMAH regulations.

Pesticides

Food and Environmental Protection Act 1995

Part III of this Act is intended to protect health and safeguard the environment in response to the use of pesticides.

Control of Pesticide Regulations 1986

These relate to the approval, advertisement, sale, supply, storage and use of pesticides. Consents with conditions are granted by MAFF. Details are published in the *Pesticides Register* (a monthly listing of UK approved pesticides and announcements) and the annual MAFF/HSE reference book.[1] Local authorities have responsibility where advertisement, sale, supply, storage and use of pesticides relates to commercial or domestic premises. The HSE has responsibility elsewhere. The aerial application of pesticides requires a certificate under the Air Navigation Order 1985, and advance notification is required to certain persons including environmental health staff as well as other requirements concerning the application.

Pollution at sea

Food and Environmental Protection Act 1995

Part II of this Act requires a licence for the disposal of waste at sea from MAFF or the minister responsible for fisheries in that area. This part of the Act also has enforcement sections.

Waste on land

Environmental Protection Act 1990

Part II of this Act deals with waste management, including disposal and provides the regulatory framework to ensure that harm to the environment is minimised. This includes both authorised and unauthorised waste disposal and treatment. Waste regulation in England and Wales is undertaken by the Environment Agency. The Scottish Environmental Protection Agency undertakes this function in Scotland.

Contaminated land

Environment Act 1995

Section 57 has added Part IIA to the Environmental Protection Act 1990. This covers identifying and dealing with contaminated land. Local authorities are the enforcing authority, and the Environment Agency or Scottish Environmental Protection Agency are responsible for designated special sites.

[1] MAFF.HSE (1997) *Pesticides Approved Under the Control of Pesticides Regulations*, 1986, London: HMSO.

Section Three

Response

The response stage commences once an incident has been recognised and lasts as long as rapid interventions are conducted. It is characterised by pressure of time, rapid decision-making (preferably according to a prearranged chain of command) and emergency responders' attempts to comply with prepared contingency plans. The role of the public health physician during this phase is to undertake health risk assessment using epidemiological methods, to define the populations at risk from different types of exposure, to rapidly collect valid data on exposure levels, and to relate these to health status information. The public health physician should also be involved in evaluating the impact of the incident and advising public health officials and the public on preventive measures.

16 General considerations

Major chemical incidents impose extraordinary pressures and demands on public health physicians and their teams. As these incidents occur only rarely, few public health physicians have gained sufficient actual experience to enable an automatic response. This section has been designed to provide a basic approach to aid the management of a public health response to a chemical incident. However, as no two incidents are identical, it is recommended that this guidance should be used flexibly to accommodate the events as they develop rather than to dictate the agenda. This guide should augment, where necessary, the existing tried and tested local emergency plan and action cards, if available, rather than replace them.

Team approach

An adequate response to a major chemical incident cannot be provided by an individual. It is important to obtain help at an early stage. This may include rescheduling other routine duties, strengthening the on-call rota, securing adequate secretarial and information technology support, and dealing with domestic arrangements.

Often, large numbers of people are willing to help and need only to be asked. Colleagues tend to prefer to be involved from the beginning of an incident – their sense of ownership towards the response to the incident will be greater than if they have been called upon as a last resort when events are threatening to overwhelm resources. Ideally, all those involved in responding to an incident should be freed from other duties until it is clear that resources are sufficient.

A cohesive, multidisciplinary response to significant events such as chemical incidents, can be difficult to sustain. Individuals comprising the response team may not have had the opportunity to work with each other previously, and may not fully understand each others' roles within the team and its aims. General and personal criticism by the press may disturb individual professional colleagues sufficiently to weaken the unity of the response. Confidentiality of proceedings and trust in each other must exist to minimise the chances of a group breaking down under pressure.

Record-keeping

The maintenance of full and accurate records of events as an incident develops is vital. For the group, detailed minutes ratified at the start of each meeting followed by an incident report will suffice. As an aid to communication, it is useful to keep a list of all those people involved with their job titles, organisations and contact numbers, accessible at all times. In particular, those who attend meetings should be easily identifiable by secretarial staff, as teams may comprise a large number of unfamiliar individuals.

A detailed contemporaneous personal record of events should also be created. This will aid the public health physician's own decision-making process and serve as a record of their role in the incident, especially when it is over and various inquiries seek to investigate the incident. Personal records can also be used to assess the public health team's role, identify where improvements can be made, and eventually disseminate information more widely to colleagues and students.

Assessment and decision-making

An acute incident requires an immediate response and assessment of the situation followed by a decision on whether or not to take action. An incident with a longer-term evolution requires immediate response and assessment, but less acute action may be appropriate. Few incidents develop into major events. It is recommended that frequent assessments of the incident are made to review its severity and likely impact on human health.

17 Managing an incident

A pro forma questionaire which can be adapted for use during an incident can be found in Appendix 3. The following information should be recorded:

- The date and time the event was notified, plus your own name and job title.
- The informant's name, position/job title, address and contact numbers.
- The nature of the site or type of premises
- The name of the site/premises, plus its full postal address including postcode
- The name and telephone number of the on-site or off-site representative of the organisation
- A brief description of the event
  - What is known to have occurred?
  - When did it occur?
  - What chemicals are thought to have been released?
  - What is the scale of the release?
  - What are the imminent problems?
  - What problems may follow?

Detailed information relating to the source and type of an incident should be obtained as soon as possible and continually updated as the incident evolves. In practice this information may be difficult to acquire quickly, but this should not delay assessment of those at risk and issuing preventive safety advice where necessary.

Characteristics of the site/premises

Background information should be obtained on the site activities and the chemicals stored on site:

- Is it a CIMAH or non–CIMAH site?
- Has it been registered by the local authority?
- What is the name of the company or person responsible for the site, with contact details, to assist in obtaining further information?
- What chemicals are stored and used on site – do any stock lists/registers exist?
- Do the site/premises have occupational health input?
- Do emergency plans already exist, and have public health issues been incorporated into them?

Characteristics of the chemicals involved

It is important to determine as accurately as possible information relating to chemical(s) which have been released and which may be still being released. This will help information sources such as the National Poisons Information Centres or the health authority's chemical incident adviser to produce a summary information sheet on each chemical. Useful information to assist this process includes:

- names of the chemical(s) – either trade or generic
- United Nations Number(s) of the chemical(s)
- Chemical Abstract Series Number(s)
- COSHH data sheet(s)
- Manufacturer's Safety Data Sheet(s)
- proper composition and breakdown of the chemical(s)

Media into which the chemicals have been released

- **Air** – influence of wind direction and other meteorological conditions on potential dispersal
- **Land** – residential, industrial, agricultural or recreational
- **Food** – for consumption by humans and/or animals, either commercially produced vegetables/livestock, home-grown produce or other non-commercially produced foodstuffs
- **Water** – drinking (human and/or animal), recreational, fishing

Characteristics of the event

The type of incident will govern the type of response required. Considerations include:

- **Fire**
  - early public awareness
  - multiple products of combustion
  - potential for widespread dispersal
  - difficulty in predicting an exact end to the event
  - run-off of contaminated water/foam
- **Explosion**
  - threat of further explosions, accidental or deliberate – this may hamper activities directed at containment
  - greater chance of requiring evacuation
- **Transport-related**
  - congestion, traffic, rail jams
  - exposure to those using transport route
  - potential for further accidents
  - possibility of explosive risk
- **Spillage**
  - direct land contamination
  - greater chance of entering watercourses
- **Inland water**
  - widespread risk to population possible
  - identification of at-risk sites: hospitals, schools, residential homes, prisons
  - identification of at-risk populations: housebound, renal dialysis patients, children, elderly

- urgent need for alternative supplies
- **Sea/coastal waters**
  - involvement of coast guard, Royal National Lifeboat Institution
  - dispersal
  - wildlife impact
  - fishing industry
  - recreational activities
  - potential for international involvement
- **Food contamination**
  - cases may be sporadic, delaying identification
  - naturally occurring toxins may be involved
  - may be malicious
- **Malicious contamination**
  - threat of further attacks
  - reliability of information being supplied
  - possibility of copy-cat attacks

Weather

Data on the current meteorological conditions are important as the effects of the weather can influence the situation with regard to:

- spread of agent(s) by winds or to waterways by rainfall
- production of by-products due to chemical interaction with rain
- potential dilution by rainfall
- potential for evaporation of volatile compounds in dry, sunny or windy conditions

Toxicology summary

Based on the chemical(s) involved and the characteristics of the event, the National Poisons Information Service or health authority chemical incident advisers may generate a toxicology summary in a format which may include some of the following:

- first aid measures
- acute management
- chronic management
- chemical properties
- potential to form toxic by-products
- antidote data
- Maximum Exposure Limit (ranging from minutes to hours) – the maximum concentration to which an employee may be exposed under any circumstances.

If available, the Occupational Exposure Standard (long-term day-after-day exposure to an airborne substance) may also prove helpful.

Ensure that a summary is made of the current knowledge of the hazards involved, and update the risk assessment. Further information will no doubt emerge, and this process should be repeated as required.

Population characteristics

Establish:

- the number of people exposed (including emergency services personnel, pregnant women, children, elderly), injured or dead
- potential for exposure
- population density, local housing, schools, hospitals, etc.
- presence of other diseases, e.g. severe respiratory and renal disease
- proximity of other industrial sites
- availability of shelter, crowds at sporting occasions, e.g. football matches
- communication difficulties, e.g. people on golf courses, deaf and/or blind
- special conditions, e.g. underground railways, road and rail tunnels

Assess the following:

- Does a significant ongoing or potential risk to the population exist?
- What is the nature of that risk?
- Could preventive measures reduce this risk?
- Would these outweigh any potential adverse consequences?

If benefits outweigh adverse effects, decide:

- Which measures to adopt
- How to implement these measures
- When to implement these measures
- Who should implement these measures

Consider the following:

- the need for population screening
- the identification of controls for any follow-up study
- the need for community counselling and dissemination of information

Communication

This is critical to the management of any incident. There are three warning periods from the start of an incident:

- First period (0–2 hours)
- Second period (2–12 hours)
- Third period (12–24 hours)

The following actions should be undertaken as rapidly as possible:

- Notify the health authority media or communications department.
- Establish communication links with allied agencies (see the checklist below), noting the following details:

- contact name
- job title
- organisation and department
- contact number
- date contacted
- time contacted.

- Update the list of contacts and circulate it to all involved within the health authority.
- Establish early agreement on the media management strategy:
  - single source of information
  - proactive approach
  - health issues to be dealt with by public health physicians with the appropriate expertise
- Establish a helpline, if appropriate.
- Ensure the affected community is given early information of the results on any planned follow-up or research.

Checklist of possible contacts

police

fire

ambulance

health authority chemical incident adviser/SCIEH

National Poisons Information Service

person or company responsible for the site

transport company, if appropriate

environmental health department

Department of Health and other government departments

National Focus

Environment Agency/Scottish Environment Protection Agency

Ministry of Agriculture, Fisheries and Food/Scottish Office Agriculture, Environment and Fisheries Department

Health and Safety Executive

water authorities

coast guard

Ensure that communications with other relevant organisations are initiated as soon as possible.

Health care resources

During an incident, decisions have to be made on the best ways to allocate and organise health care resources. Any reorganisation within acute health care facilities is largely a matter for the provider unit responding to the event. However, there may be occasions when urgent purchasing arrangements have to be made with neighbouring trusts or national centres, for example those with burns units or hyperbaric oxygen units.

The creation of a register of affected individuals may assist in the planned, temporary restructuring of health care services, will facilitate in the preparation of press releases and will aid future epidemiological studies. For each accident and emergency department responding to an incident a register should be created based on established emergency procedures. It should at least be able to provide the following information at short notice:

- the number of casualties attending
- the number of people in special groups, e.g. children, old people
- classification of the severity of injuries – this should correspond to the coloured-label triage system[1]
- **P1** – red – needs immediate resuscitation
- **P2** – yellow – urgent treatment needed
- **P3** – green – needs treatment but can wait
- **P4** – black/white – dead or expected death

- types of injury – burns, fractures, etc.
- number of admissions
- need to redirect other casualties
- use of decontamination facilities
- need for supplies of antidote
- need for additional A&E resources
- need for additional inpatient facilities
- need for specialist facilities, e.g. burns unit

Efforts should be made to identify individuals who attend A&E departments outside their district of residence.

Basic information on those attending their general practitioners should also be obtained and added to the register, but there may be delays in obtaining this data. Regional and national advice and surveillance units such as the National Poisons Information Service, the health authority's chemical incident adviser, the National Focus and the Scottish Centre for Infection and Environmental Health may have a role in helping to collate incident-related information from a wide variety of sources.

Epidemiological follow-up

In order to undertake long-term epidemiological follow-up, further information will be required, including:

- demographic details
- identification of high-risk groups
- medical history:
  - symptoms
  - signs
- results of clinical investigations

- classification of exposure status
  - proximity
  - length of exposure
  - presence of protective clothing
  - state of clothes, clothing specimens, skin swabs
  - clinical condition
- data from long-term clinical follow-up

A sample information collection form to collect individuals' data can be found in Appendix 4.

Epidemiological study

A range of options may be considered, depending on the exact circumstances of the incident; the final choice will depend on scientific, political and resource constraints. To facilitate the decision-making process, a report including a review of literature, results of consultations with the public addressing their fears, concerns and questions, and identification of the skills and financial resources is required. Finance may be available from the insurance cover of the person or company involved. Make proper arrangements at chief executive level.

When it has been agreed to undertake an epidemiological study the following considerations are important:

- Seek local ethics committee approval before undertaking study.
- Keep the community informed using immediate 'hot' debriefs or planned debriefs as appropriate.
- The community should be the first to know the results of any investigation.
- If funding has been obtained from those responsible for the incident or with their agreement, ensure that the results can be published independently.

[1] For further information, refer to *Chemical Incident Management for Accident and Emergency Clinicians*, (1999), London: The Stationery Office.

18 Clusters

Guidelines for approach

Much of this chapter is derived from Centres for Disease Control and Prevention guidelines.[1]

A schematic representation of the process can be found in figure 3.

Initial contact

The aim of this phase is to collect information from person(s) reporting perceived health events (an initial cluster data collection form can be found in Appendix 6).

- Record the name and contact details of the caller, and the organisation (if any) to which the caller is linked.
- Record initial data relating to suspected health event(s) and putative causative exposure(s).
- Record identifying information on persons reported as affected (this may be done over a number of contacts with different people).
- Discuss impressions with the caller, stressing a number of important points:
  - a variety of diagnoses is not suggestive of a common origin
  - cancer is common, with a 1 in 4 lifetime risk This increases with age (cases among older people are less likely to be true clusters) and with activities such as tobacco smoking
  - if a type of cancer affects a specific body site in a number of people, this is a stronger indication of a cluster, especially if they are rare cancers
  - major birth defects are less common than cancer but do occur in 1–2% of live births
  - the length of time in residence or at the exposure location would have to be substantial to implicate a plausible carcinogen due to the long latent period of most known carcinogens
  - purported fatal exposures/cases may not prove helpful, as there will be a lack of information on exposure and possible confounding factors
  - even if rare diseases do cluster and appear to be statistically significant, this may be a statistical phenomenon unrelated to any exposure
- Obtain further information on cases.
- Assure the caller they will receive a written response.
- Maintain a log of all contacts relating to a particular cluster/event.
- Inform the health authority media relations department.

If assessment of information from initial contact suggests further investigation is needed, e.g. a single rare disease, plausible exposure or clustering, begin the **preliminary evaluation**.

Figure 3 Cluster investigation scheme

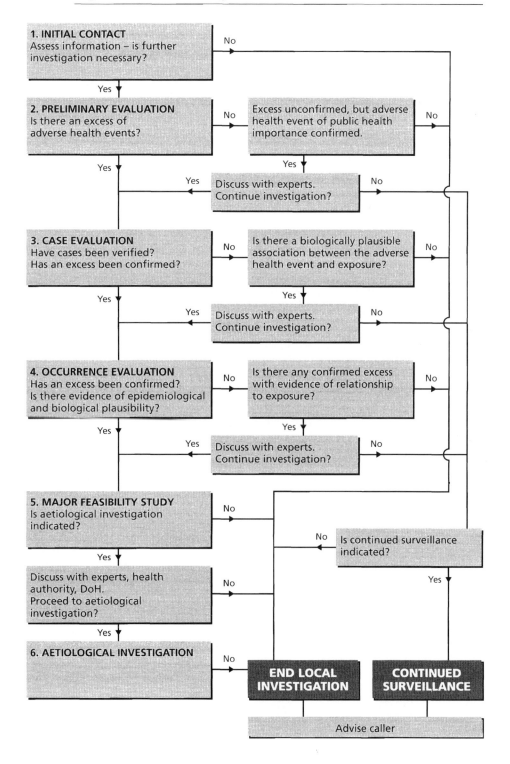

This figure was created by DJ Irwin, based on CDC *Guidelines for Investigating Clusters of Health Events*, MMWR 1990; 39; (No. RR-11) pp. 1–23.

Preliminary evaluation

The aim of this phase is to provide a quick, rough estimate of the likelihood that an important health event has occurred.

- Identify the geographic area and time period involved.
- Identify which cases are to be included in the evaluation.
  - Assume all health events are real.
  - It may prove helpful to tabulate frequencies and look at related descriptive statistics.

Identify an appropriate reference population. If there is a sufficient number of cases and a denominator can be identified, calculation of occurrence rates or mortality ratios may be possible. Compare the rates between the suspect cluster and reference populations. If sample numbers are not large, seek advice from experts in small–area health statistics.

Possible data sources include:

- population statistics
- classification of disease
- mortality statistics
- cancer registrations
- congenital malformation registrations
- hospital discharge statistics
- infectious disease statistics
- morbidity statistics from primary care
- sickness absences and occupational disease statistics
- special registers/surveys
- National Poisons Information Service/health authority chemical incident adviser

It is important to consider:

- accessibility of data
- validity of data – subject characteristics
  - medical considerations
  - administrative considerations
- completeness of data

If this exercise suggests an excess occurrence of a health event, begin the **case evaluation**.

If this exercise suggests no excess, contact the caller (and the health authority media relations officer) outlining the findings and advise that no further investigation is required.

If the exercise indicates no excess but the data suggest an occurrence of a health event which may be of public health importance, decide whether further investigation is warranted: discussion with experts is advisable in these circumstances.

Case evaluation

The aim of this phase is to verify the diagnosis and hence form a case definition.

- Consider forming an advisory group.
- Seek the patients' consent to examine their medical records.
- Contact the clinicians responsible for the patients, and consult health event registers if available.
- Obtain copies of relevant records, including pathology reports.
- Consider whether it is necessary to repeat histological examination.

If cases are verified and an excess is confirmed, begin the **occurrence evaluation**.

If some of the cases are not verified and an excess is not confirmed, contact the caller and the health authority media relations officer outlining the findings, and advise that no further investigation is required.

If some cases are not verified but there is a biologically plausible association between the alleged adverse health event and purported exposure, and data are suggestive of a small excess, consider continued surveillance of the event: discussion with experts is advisable in these circumstances.

Occurrence evaluation

The aim of this phase is to design and perform a thorough investigation to determine if an excess of health effects has occurred, and to describe the epidemiological characteristics.

- Form an advisory group, if this has not already been done.
- Agree appropriate geographical and temporal boundaries.
- Carry out rigorous case ascertainment within these boundaries.
- Decide on appropriate numerators and denominators.
- Identify the epidemiological and statistical procedures to be used to describe and analyse data.
- Perform an in-depth review of the literature.
- Consider the epidemiological and biological plausibility of the purported association.
- Assess the likelihood that an event–exposure relationship may be established.
- Assess the community's perceptions, reactions and needs.
- Complete the descriptive investigation.
- Consider seeking the local Ethics Committee's approval. This may reassure potential study subjects and their medical advisers.

If an excess is confirmed and both epidemiological and biological plausibility are strong, begin the **major feasibility study**.

If an excess is confirmed but no relationship to the purported exposure is evident, contact the caller and the health authority media relations officer outlining the findings and advise that no further investigation is required.

If an excess is not confirmed, contact the caller and health authority media relations officer outlining the findings, and advise that no further investigation is required.

Major feasibility study

The aim of this phase is to determine the feasibility of performing an epidemiological study linking the health event(s) and a putative exposure: discussion with experts is advisable in these circumstances.

- Form an advisory group, if this has not already been done.

- Review the detailed literature search, with particular emphasis on known and putative causes of the health outcome(s) of concern.

- Consider the appropriate study design(s) and their costs and expected outcomes
  - sample size
  - use of previously identified cases
  - study area and time
  - control selection

- Decide which data are to be collected on both cases and controls, including clinical and laboratory measurements.

- Discuss with the chemical incident adviser, local environmental health officers and statutory environmental protection agencies whether environmental measurements are necessary and the methods to be adopted.

- Define and gather exposure data, or a proxy for these.

- Consider the logistics of data collection and processing.

- Decide on an appropriate plan of analysis, including hypotheses to be tested and statistical power.

- Consider the potential impact of any findings on the local community and on the wider medical and political arena.

- Estimate the resource implications and requirements of the work.

- Consider seeking the local Ethics Committee's approval. This may reassure potential study subjects and their medical advisers.

If this study suggests that an **aetiological investigation** is necessary, it is likely to prove very expensive. Discuss with experts, the chief executive of the health authority, local authority representatives, the DoH/SODoH, and local and national political officials to determine the organisation best placed to conduct any investigation, and the resourcing of any investigation.

If this study suggests that little will be gained from an aetiological investigation, produce a report on behalf of the advisory group. There may be intense public and media demands for further investigation. The added weight of a group report coupled with previous efforts to develop community relationships and media contacts should help achieve an appropriate public health response.

Aetiological investigation

The aim of this phase is to perform aetiological investigation(s) of potential relationships between disease/symptom grouping(s) and exposure(s).

- Using the outcomes of the major feasibility study, develop protocols and implement any research projects. It is unlikely that this study will specifically investigate the initial cluster.

- Agree ownership of data and authorship of future publications with the organisation commissioned to undertake the research.

The investigation results should contribute to public health knowledge, either by demonstrating an association or non-association between exposure and disease, or by confirming previous studies' findings, thus allowing public health action to be taken.

[1] CDC (1990) 'Guidelines for investigating clusters of health events.' *Morbidity and Mortality Weekly Report*, **39:** (RR-11) pp. 1–23.

Section Four

Recovery

The recovery phase lasts as long as the effects of the incident can be expected to persist. Generally, more time is available to make decisions than in the response phase. However, public and political pressure may place time constraints on studies into possible health consequences of the incident. Once the response phase is over, victims start the process of coping with the repercussions of the incident, and communities tend to return to their usual activities and lose interest in the incident and its consequences.

19 Review and audit

Most chemical incidents need to be assessed and reviewed in order to understand the sequence of events and to develop better strategies for future management. Debriefing, immediate or planned, may be the most important exercise following an incident, so it should be planned for and resources allocated at the outset. An audit of the response to a chemical incident is useful in order to determine the method and manner of the response, as well as its appropriateness. It offers an opportunity to formalise lessons learnt and to provide a framework for feeding them back into the planning for any further event. It is essential that adequate documentation and report-writing is available for audit.

Suitable audit measures include:

- early recognition and response to the incident
- identification and control of the source of the incident and chemicals involved
- identification and control of routes of contamination, i.e. environmental and person-to-person
- comprehensive identification of those affected
- identification and elimination of risk factors that may have contributed to the incident

Task 1: Preparation

Structure

- Was a health authority chemical incident response plan in place?
- Was the plan drawn up in consultation with the health emergency planning adviser, the relevant chief environmental health officer and the appropriate hospital trust representative or provider unit manager?
- Were the protocols for chemical incidents a natural extension of those used for the major disaster plan?
- Were the protocols for significant chemical incidents a natural extension of those used for minor chemical incidents?
- Were additional resources, such as staff, rooms, communications equipment and computers available if needed?
- Was there a contract with a chemical incident advisory service for the health authority in place?

Process

- Have individual roles been defined, e.g. the lead person for dealing with chemical incidents?
- Did protocols cover nights, weekends and holidays?
- How often were the protocols updated?
- Did all those likely to be responsible for incident management understand their roles?

Outcome

- Has a chemical incident simulation exercise been carried out? If so, with what result?
- Was there an awareness of where plans were kept in different departments?

Task 2: Incident awareness

Structure

- Was there a system in place for the chemical incident response provider, the A&E departments, GPs and other physicians in the district to inform the consultant in communicable disease control/consultant in public health medicine as soon as they saw cases related to a possible chemical incident?
- Did this system incorporate chronic as well as acute exposure?

Process

- Did the consultant in communicable disease contral/consultant in public health medicine record and monitor cases to allow detection of an abnormal distribution/cluster?

Outcome

- Was the average notification interval known for the different groups of informants?

Task 3: Initial investigation

Structure

- What information was sought in the initial investigation?
- Was there a pro forma questionnaire available for use?
- Who collected the information, and on what authority?

Process

- What documentation was obtained and how maintained?
- Was it collected on all susceptible cases?
- What samples, if any, were taken?
- How was information from the field relayed to the co-ordinating centre?
- Were minutes distributed prior to the next meeting?

Outcome

- How long did it take to collect initial information?
- Did this information prove to be valid?
- What action was taken on the basis of the initial information?

Task 4: Incident control group

Structure

- Who called the group together and in what circumstances?
- Who chaired the incident control group? Was this agreed in advance?

- Did the composition of the group reflect appropriate and sufficient expertise for the management of the incident?
- Was a press officer designated?

Process

- Were all members of the group clear about their roles?
- Were the roles stated on an action card?
- Were meetings attended by all who were required?
- Were meetings minuted?

Outcome

- Were incident control group decisions acted upon fully?

Task 5: Epidemiological investigation

Structure

- Did the investigation include active case-finding of exposed individuals?
- Were exposure histories available and used?
- Were questions asked by phone, post or face-to-face interviews?
- Were the questionnaires validated?

Process

- What proportion of known cases were questioned?
- Were controls used?
- Was a computer used for data handling and analysis?

Outcome

- Was the source of the incident identified and were the immediate health effects documented?

Task 6: Control and management procedures

Structure

- Were there hospital decontamination protocols in place to minimise the risk of secondary contamination of health care workers?
- Was there a policy on antidote provision?
- Were there procedures in place for the taking and storing of biological samples?

Process

- Did the procedures in place for decontamination, antidote provision and biological sample collection work smoothly?

Outcome

- How many cases of health care worker with secondary contamination arose despite the control measures?
- How many of the samples taken were analysed?

Task 7: Communication

Structure

- Were communications procedures set out in the basic protocols?
- Did they include communications with local agencies, the media and the public?
- Were there facilities for a helpline, if required?

Process

- Was the procedure followed?

Outcome

- Were there difficulties in managing the incident due to problems with communication?

Task 8: Completing an incident (recovery)

Structure

- Was there a procedure in place for declaring the incident over?
- Has the need for further monitoring and surveillance been identified and have procedures been put in place?

Process

- Was the outbreak documented or written up for publication?
- Has legal action been considered by the statutory authorities?
- Has any action been taken to reduce the risk of a similar incident?

Outcome

- Were staff and other resources available for other work?
- Was the human distress resulting from this incident the least possible?
- Have any lessons learnt led to review of plans?
- Has any legal action been taken against the health authority? If so, what was the outcome?

20 Case follow-up/incidence surveillance

Follow-up of exposed and affected individuals or potential clusters is likely to be a long-term activity. Much of the preparatory work necessary to undertake this has been described in sections Two and Three. Close liaison with experts in the field of long-term, potentially large-scale surveillance of exposed and affected individuals or potential clusters is essential. The development of systems for the storage, retrieval and analysis of this data can be complex. When such systems are to be held by a health authority, advice on compliance with the requirements of the Data Protection Act 1984 should be sought.

21 Report production

Accurately recorded contemporaneous information is the basis of any incident report. Such data may also prove essential in the event of a subsequent public enquiry or legal action.

A brief summary report of most incidents will be important for a review of the public health response. Often a short commentary on the sequence of events and any actions taken will be sufficient. However, more detailed reports are invaluable, especially when documenting complex events which have had a significant health impact. All public health physicians are well trained in report-writing. In chemical incident reports, public health physicians should seek to include material from other agencies involved in the response:

- Fire service reports may include information on the wind direction, and thus direction of plumes.
- Local or national weather station wind and meteorological data may support the information obtained from fire service reports.
- Environmental health departments may be able to provide information relating to exposure data concerning atmospheric pollution, land contamination and may also be involved in drinking water contamination incidents.
- The water supply industry may be able to provide information on events which lead to drinking water contamination.
- The Environment Agency/Scottish Environment Protection Agency may be able to provide data on any water pollution incident, land contamination and some atmospheric pollution.
- The Health and Safety Executive may provide information where they are the enforcement authority.

This information may help to determine the significance, by time and place, of adverse health effects from local hospitals, general practitioners and pharmacists.

Most public health physicians undertake literature searches as a routine activity. Data is available in textbooks, journals, CD-ROMS and the Internet (see Appendix 1 and the bibliography). Search strategies need to be defined to enable the appropriate data to be obtained. If toxicological assessments are required expert advice should be sought from the National Poisons Information Service or the health authority's chemical incident adviser.

Reports should contain a non-technical executive summary, a description of the evolution of the incident, literature review, case definition, methods, results, discussion, conclusions and recommendations. Any lessons on effective response activities should be drawn as well as on those that did not proceed effectively. These lessons should be reviewed in the light of the health authority emergency plan. Publication of responses to important incidents in the medical literature will assist other public health departments in preparing their plans and responses.

Appendices

1 Sources of information

Emergency 24-hour telephone numbers: National Poisons Information Service

Belfast	01232 240503
Birmingham	0121 507 5588
Cardiff	01222 709901
Dublin	(+353) 1 837 9964 or (+353) 1 837 9966
Edinburgh	0131 536 2300
Leeds	0113 234 0715
London	0171 635 9191
Newcastle upon Tyne	0191 232 5131

Chemical incident provider units

London, South East, Eastern, North West, Trent, South and **West.** Health authorities in these regions are contracted with the Chemical Incident Response Service at the Medical Toxicology Unit, Guy's and St Thomas' Hospital Trust, Avonley Road, London SE14 5ER. Tel. 0171 771 5383. Fax. 0171 771 5363. 24-hour emergency via NPIS: Tel. 0171 635 9191. Fax. 0171 771 5309.

West Midlands. Health authorities in this region are contracted with the Chemical Hazard Management and Research Centre at the Institute of Public and Environmental Health, University of Birmingham, Birmingham B15 2TT. Tel. 0121 414 3985/6547. Fax. 0121 414 3827/3630. 24-hour emergency Tel. 0171 394 5112.

Northern and **Yorkshire Region.** Health authorities in this region are contracted with the Chemical Incident Service at The Department of Environmental and Occupational Medicine, The Medical School, University of Newcastle, Newcastle Upon Tyne NE2 4HH. Tel. 0191 222 7195. Fax. 0191 222 6442.

Scotland. Scottish Centre for Infection and Environmental Health at Clifton House, Clifton Place, Glasgow G3 7LN. Tel. 0141 300 1100. Fax. 0141 300 1170. Covers all health authorities in Scotland.

Wales and **Northern Ireland.** Health authorities in these areas are contracted with the Chemical Incident Management Support Unit at University of Wales College of Medicine, Therapeutics and Toxicology Centre, Llandough Hospital, Cardiff CF64 2XX. Tel. 01222 709901. 24-hour emergency: Tel. 01222 715278.

Public health laboratories

Belfast Regional Poisons Information Centre, Royal Victoria Hospital, Grosvenor Road, Belfast BT12 6BA. Tel. 01232 240503.

Birmingham Regional Laboratory for Toxicology, City Road Hospital, PO Box 293, Birmingham B18 7QH. *Trace elements*: Tel. 0121 554 9137. *Solvents, pesticides, drugs etc*: Tel. 0121 507 4135.

Cardiff Welsh National Poisons Unit, Gwenwyn Ward, Llandough Hospital, Penarth, Vale of Glamorgan CF64 2XX. *Solvents, pesticides, drugs etc.*: Tel. 01222 711 711 extension 5154/5197.

Glasgow Trace Elements Reference Laboratory, MacEwan Building, Glasgow Royal Infirmary, Glasgow G4 0SF. *Trace elements*: Tel. 0141 211 4256.

Guildford Trace Element Reference Centre, Department of Clinical Biochemistry & Clinical Nutrition, Robens Institute, University of Surrey, Guildford GU2 5XH. *Trace elements*: Tel. 01483 259220.

London Trace Metals Laboratory, Department of Clinical Biochemistry, King's College Hospital, Denmark Hill, London SE5 9RS. *Trace elements*: Tel. 0171 737 4000. Medical Toxicology Unit, New Cross, Avonley Road, London SE14 5ER. *Trace elements*: Tel. 0171 635 1060. *Solvents, pesticides, drugs etc.*: Tel. 0171 635 1050 or 0171 635 1058. *Non-biological material*: Tel. 0171 635 1060.

Newcastle upon Tyne Analytical Chemistry Unit, Department of Environmental and Occupational Medicine, Medical School, University of Newcastle, Newcastle upon Tyne NE2 4HH. *Non-biological material*: Tel. 0191 222 7015 or 0191 222 7255.

Southampton Trace Element Unit, Chemical Pathology Dept, Inst. of Human Nutrition, Southampton General Hospital, Tremona Road, Southampton SO16 6YO. *Trace elements*: Tel. 01703 796419. Fax. 01703 796294.

Teddington Laboratory of the Government Chemist, Queens Road, Teddington Middlesex TW11 0LY. *Non-biological material*: Tel. 0181 943 7000.

The health authority chemical advice provider or the National Focus should be able to advise on the battery of analyses each laboratory can perform. Contact the laboratories for estimates of cost and specific sampling instructions.

Public analyst laboratories

A network of 33 public analyst laboratories is subsumed under the umbrella of The Association of Public Analysts, Burlington House, Piccadilly, London W1V 0BN. Your local laboratory can be identified via the Yellow Pages under 'Public Analysts', 'Laboratory Facilities' or 'Chemists, Analytical and Research'.

Most laboratories serve more than one local authority. For a fee they will undertake chemical analyses of contaminants in air, soil, water, effluents, run–off, soil, spills, sediments, foods, ash and waste, contaminated land investigation and site surveys with risk and hazard assessment on behalf of statutory authorities on either an urgent or non–urgent basis.

Local

Local sources of information are the most useful in providing support and resources for chemical incident prevention and response. This list is not exhaustive but indicates the wide range of agencies which may have a role in a chemical incident:

- emergency services (police, fire and ambulance service)
- local health professionals including general practitioners and hospital staff, in particular those in accident and emergency departments
- local government and environmental health departments including emergency planning officers, environmental health officers, housing department and trading standards officers
- local officers or inspectors of the EA/SEPA, the HSE and the MAFF/SOAEFD

National

Below are some of the relevant governmental departments and agencies. Other organisations, including university departments and institutes with medical toxicology, surveillance and environmental interests, voluntary agencies, societies and international agencies may also be useful. Any additional information required is likely to be available from the National Focus or the health authorities' chemical incident adviser.

Government departments and agencies:

CEFAS Remembrance Avenue, Burnham on Crouch, Essex CMO 8HA. Tel. 01621 787200.

Communicable Disease Surveillance Centre 61 Colindale Avenue, London NW9 5EQ. Tel. 0181 200 6868.

Department of the Environment Transport and the Regions Eland House, Bressenden Place, London SW1E 5DU. Tel. 0171 890 3000.

Department of Health 79 Whitehall, London SW1A 2NS. Tel. 0171 210 4850 (information service 10am to 4pm). Switchboard: 0171 210 3000.

Department of Trade and Industry 1 Victoria Street, London SW1H OET. Tel. 0171 215 5000.

Department of Transport Great Minster House, 76 Marsham Street, London SW1P 4DR. (Tel. 0171 271 4800). General enquiries 0171 890 3000.

Environment Agency Romney House, 43 Marsham Street, London SW1P 3PY. Tel. 0171 890 3000.

Health and Safety Executive Rose Court, 2 Southwark Bridge, London, SE1 9HS. Tel. 0171 717 6000.

Home Office 50 Queen Anne's Gate, London SW1H 9AT. Tel. 0171 273 4000.

Laboratory of the Government Chemist Queens Road, Teddington, Middlesex TW11 0LY. Tel. 0181 943 7000.

Marine Pollution Control Unit Spring Place, 105 Commercial Road, Southampton SO15 1EG. Tel. 01703 329412/407. 24 hour hotline for incidents 01703 329415.

Medicines Control Agency Market Towers, 19 Elms Lane, Vauxhall, London SW8 5NQ. Tel. 0171 273 0000 or 0171 273 0451.

Ministry of Defence Whitehall, London SW1A 2HB. Tel. 0171 218 9000.

Ministry of Agriculture, Fisheries and Food: Veterinary Medicines Directorate Woodham Lane, New Haw, Addlestone, Weybridge KT15 3LS. Tel. 01932 336911.

National Chemical Emergency Centre Culham, Didcot, Oxfordshire OX14 3DB. Tel. 01235 463060.

National Radiological Protection Board Chiltern, Didcot, Oxfordshire OX11 ORQ. Tel. 01235 831600. 24 hour emergency number: Tel. 01235 834590.

Office for National Statistics 1 Drummond Gate, London SW1V 2QQ. Tel. 0171 533 5257. Cancer stats. general enquiries 0171 533 6363.

Regional Drug Therapeutics Centre Wolfson Unit, Claremont Place, Newcastle upon Tyne NE2 4HH. Tel: 0191 232 1525.

Scottish Centre for Infection and Environmental Health Clifton House, Clifton Place, Glasgow G3 7LM. Tel. 0141 300 1100.

Other Agencies

British Association for Counselling 1 Regent Place, Rugby, Warwickshire CV21 2PJ. Tel. 01788 550899.

Fire Research Establishment Moreton-in-the-Marsh, Gloucester GL56 ORH. Tel. 01608 50831.

Fire Service Training College Tel. 01608 650831.

Health and Safety Executive: Pesticide Incident Appraisal Panel Rose Court, 2 Southwark Bridge, London SE1 9HS. Tel. 0171 717 6000.

Major Hazard Incident Data Service, AEA Technology, Thomson House, Risley, Warrington WA3 6AT. Tel. 01925 254486.

Relate National Office, Herbert Gray College, Little Church Street, Rugby, Warwickshire CV21 3AT. Tel. 01788 573241.

Royal Botanic Gardens Centre for Economic Botany, Banks Building, Kew Richmond, Surrey TW9 3AB. Tel. 0181 332 5702.

Waste Management Information Bureau AEA Technology plc, F6, Culham, Abingdon, Oxfordshire OX14 3DB. Tel. 01235 463162. Fax 01235 463004.

Water Research Centre Henley Road, Medmenham, Marlow, Buckinghamshire SL7 2HD. Tel. 01491 571531. Fax 01491 579094.

University departments and institutes

Centre for Occupational Health, School of Epidemiology and Health Sciences, University of Manchester Stopford Building, Oxford Road, Manchester M13 9PT. Tel. 0161 275 5522.

Centres For Toxicology, Environmental Biotechnology, and Environmental Strategy, University of Surrey Guildford, Surrey GU2 5XH. Tel. 01483 300800.

The Chartered Institute of Environmental Health Chadwick Court, 15 Hatfield, London SE1 8DJ. Tel. 0171 928 6006.

Department of Environmental & Occupational Medicine and Epidemiology & Public Health, University of Newcastle The Medical School, Newcastle upon Tyne NE2 4HH. Tel. 0191 222 6000.

Department of Public Health and Environment and Institute of Occupational Health, University of Birmingham Edgbaston, Birmingham B15 2TT. Tel. 0121 414 6030.

Department of Toxicology Wolfson Institute, Charterhouse Square, London EC1M 6BQ. Tel. 0171 982 6126.

Department of Environmental & Preventive Medicine, St. Bartholomew's Medical College, University of London, Wolfson Institute, Charterhouse Square, London, EC1M 6BQ Tel: 0171 982 6269.

Emergency Planning College Easingwold, Yorkshire YO61 3EG. Tel. 01347 821406.

Faculty of Occupational Medicine 6 St Andrew's Place, Regents Park, London NW1 4LB. Tel. 0171 317 5890.

Institute for the Environment & Health, University of Leicester 94 Regents Road, Leicester LE1 7DD. Tel. 0116 223 1600.

Mathematical Sciences Division, School of Informantics, University of Abertay, Dundee Bell Street, Dundee. Tel. 01382 308604. E-mail: a.lawson@tay.ac.uk or a.clark@tay.ac.uk

Robens Centre for Health Ergonomics, University of Surrey Guildford GU2 5XH. Tel. 01483 259203.

School of Environmental Sciences and Community Care, Cardiff Institute of Higher Education Western Avenue, Llandaff, Cardiff CF5 2YB. Tel. 01222 551111.

Small Area Health Statistics Unit Department of Epidemiology and Public Health, Imperial College of Science, Technology and Medicine, London. Tel. 0171 589 5111.

South East Institute of Public Health, Environmental Health Department, University of London Broomhill House, David Saloman's Estate, Broomhill Road, Tonbridge Wells, Kent TN3 OXT. Tel. 01892 515153.

WHO Collaborating Centre for Environmental Health Promotion & Ecology, Department of Social Medicine, University of Bristol Canynge Hall, Whiteladies Road, Bristol BS1 2NT. Tel. 0117 928 7279.

WHO Collaborating Centre for Health in Employment and the Environment Dr. Robin Philipp, Department of Occupational Health and Safety, Bristol Royal Infirmary, Bristol BS2 8HW. Tel. 0117 928 2352. Fax: 0117 928 3840.

Voluntary agencies

British Red Cross National Office, 9 Grosvenor Crescent, London SW1X 7EJ. Tel. 0171 235 5454.

St John Ambulance Brigade Headquarters, 1 Grosvenor Crescent, London SW1X 7EF. Tel. 0171 235 5231.

Samaritans Central London Office (admin. only), 46 Marshall Street, London W1V 1LR. Tel. 0171 439 1406.

Scottish Woman's Royal Voluntary Service 44 Albany Street, Edinburgh EH1 3QR. Tel. 0131 558 8028.

Women's Royal Voluntary Service Milton Hill House, Milton Hill, Abingdon, Oxfordshire OX13 6AF. Tel. 01235 442900.

Societies

British Medical Association BMA House, Tavistock Square, London WC1H 9JP. Tel. 0171 387 4499.

British Occupational Hygiene Society Suite 2, Georgian House, Great Northern Road, Derby DE1 1LT. Tel. 01332 298101.

British Toxicology Society: Human Section Sub-Group Institute of Biology, 20 Queensbury Place, London SW7 2D2. Tel. 0171 581 8333.

European Association of Poisons Centres CH1211, 20 Avenue Appia, Geneva 27, Switzerland. Tel. (+41) 22 791 21 11.

International Society of Toxicology Zentrum der Rechtsmedizin, Kennedy Allee 104, D 60596, Frankfurt, Germany.

Public Health Medicine Environment Group c/o Faculty of Public Health Medicine, 4 St Andrews Place, Regents Park, London NW1 4LB. Tel: 0171 933 0243.

Research Committee on Disasters University of Delaware, Newark DE1 9716. USA.

Royal Society of Chemistry Thomas Graham House, Science Park, Milton Road Cambridge CB4 0WF. Tel. 01223 420066.

Society of Industrial Emergency Services Officers 11 Court House Gardens Lower Cam, Dursley GL11 5LP. Tel. 01453 549225.

International agencies

Agency for Toxic Substances and Disease Registry 1600 Clifton Road, NE (E-28), Atlanta GA 30333. Tel. (+1) 404 639 0727.

Centers for Disease Control and Prevention 1600 Clifton Road, NE, Atlanta GA 30333. Tel. (+1) 404 332 4555.

International Commission on Occupational Health Department of Community, Occupational & Family Medicine, National University Hospital, Lower Kent Ridge Road, 119074, Republic of Singapore. Tel. (+65) 772 4290.

International Programme on Chemical Safety (WHO/ILO/UNEP) 20 Avenue Appia, CH1211, Geneva 27, Switzerland. Tel. (+41) 22 791 21 11.

United Nations Environment Programme Industry And Environment Programme Activity Centre, 39–43 Quai André Citroën, 75739 Paris, France CEDEX 15. Tel. (+33) 1 44 37 14 50.

Electronic resources

Databases useful in toxicology

A full list with descriptions is available from the Guy's and St Thomas' Medical Toxicology Unit Library. The unit has access to the following and will provide searches on request (the cost of a search would start at £30).

The following databases have been selected as being the most useful overall, balancing price and the amount of information each contains.

Key: B = bibliographic only; F = factual information on toxicology and health effects

1 **Current Contents** (B): This is a current awareness service available on floppy disk, updated weekly. Several different standards of this service are available, including abstracts.

2 **Excerpta Medica** (B): 1974 to date. Biomedical literature, concentrating on European sources, emphasis on pharmacological effects of drugs and chemicals. Author abstracts for 65% of articles, selected from 4,500 journals.

3 **Medline** (B): 1966 to date. Over six million records; the electronic version of Index Medicus. Author abstracts for about 70% of items, indexing from 3,000 journals.

4 **Poisindex** (F): Extensive series of monographs aimed at medical and informed professionals describing how to deal with intoxications from the whole range of toxic substances. Includes clinical treatment, signs and symptoms, characteristics of the substance, analysis and reference to any previous known cases.

5 **Registry of Toxic Effects of Chemical Substances** (F): Toxicity data from the scientific literature; includes known toxic substances which are mined, manufactured, processed, synthesised or naturally occurring. Compiled by the National Institute for Occupational Safety and Health.

6 **Toxline** (B): 1965 to date. Comprises material from Medline and 15 other databases, covering published material and research in progress in adverse drug reactions, carcinogenesis, mutagenesis, teratogenesis, environmental pollution, etc. Over one million documents.

7 **HazDat** (F) (Hazardous Substance Release/Health Effects Database); Compiled by the Agency for Toxic Substances and Disease Registry (USA).

8 **Toxicological Profiles** (F): Compiled by The Agency for Toxic Substances and Disease Registry (USA). Available on CD-ROM.

Other databases are also available for the emergency services.

Toxicology Internet and World Wide Web sites

Over the past three or four years these sites have changed frequently. Those given below were correct at the time of going to press.

The Agency for Toxic Substances and Disease Registry (USA) home page carries information compiled by the ATSDR including: HazDat profiles, toxico-logical profiles, chemical-specific fact sheets, plus other information: http://atsdr1.atsdr.cdc.gov:8080/atsdrhome.html

The Chemical Industry Institute of Toxicology has one of the most comprehensive sites and regularly updates its list of web sites of biological, chem-ical and environmental interest: http://www.ciit.org

The Institute for Environmental Toxicology (USA) home page can be found at: http:www.iet.msu.edu

The Venom and Toxins Research Group at the University of Singapore have a bilingual (English/Chinese) database, including a directory of venoms and poisons, and lists of antivenoms, Poison Control Centres and toxicologists around the world: http://vhp.nus.sg

2 Antidotes and supportive therapies

The following antidotes and supportive therapies should be available for immediate use.

Key:

G = general antidote

R = routinely held antidote

E = emergency kit antidote

SC = specialist centre antidote

General

ACTIVATED CHARCOAL (G)
Use: Non-specific adsorbent

BRONCHODILATORS (G)
Use: Respiratory support

NEBULIZED STEROIDS (G)
Use: Respiratory support

OXYGEN (G)
Use: Respiratory support

Examples of toxic substances and antidotes

ARSENIC
Antidote: See 'metals' below.

BISMUTH
Antidote: See 'metals' below.

CARBAMATE PESTICIDES
Antidote: Atropine (E)

CARBON TETRACHLORIDE
Antidote: N-acetyl cysteine

COPPER
Antidote: See 'metals' below.

CYANIDE
Antidote: Amyl nitrite, (E, first aid only)
liquid sodium thiosulphate (E,R)
sodium nitrite (E,R)
dicobalt edetate (R)

ETHYLENE GLYCOL
Antidote: Absolute alcohol (R)

HYDROFLUORIC ACID
Antidote: Calcium gluconate (E,R)

INSECTICIDES
See 'Organophosphorus pesticides' and 'Carbamate pesticides'.

LEAD
Antidote: Succimer (DMSA) (SC)

MERCURY
Antidote: See 'metals' below.

METALS
Antidote: Sodium 2,3-dimercapto-1-
propanesulphonate (DMPS) (SC).
Also three chelating agents:
Dimercaprol (Hg, Pb, As),
Penicillamine (Pb, Cu, As) and
sodium calcium edetate (Pb) (R)

METHANOL
Antidote: Absolute alcohol (R)

NITRATES, NITRITES
Antidote: Methylene blue (R)

NITROBENZENE (DAPSONE, LIGNOCAINE, SULPHONAMIDES, BENZOCAINE)
Antidote: Methylene blue (R)

ORGANOPHOSPHORUS PESTICIDES
Antidote: Atropine (E, SC),
pralidoxime mesylate (SC)

THALLIUM
Antidote: Berlin blue (SC)

Radioactive isotopes

PLUTONIUM AND OTHER ACTINIDES
Antidote: Diethylene triamine penta-a-acetic acid
held by the nuclear industry and EDTA (R)

RADIOCAESIUM
Antidote: Prussian blue (R)

RADIOIODINE
Antidote: Potassium iodate (stable
iodine) held by the nuclear industry (SC)

Pharmaceutical agents

DIGOXIN
Antidote: Digoxin-specific antibody fragments (SC)

ANTIPSYCHOTIC DRUGS (extrapyramidal effects)
Antidote: Procyclidine, benztropine (R)

PARACETAMOL
Antidote: N–acetyl cysteine, methionine, (R)

METHOTREXATE
Antidote: Folinic acid (R)

BETA–BLOCKING AGENTS
Antidote: Glucagon (R)

OPIOIDS
Antidote: Naloxone (E,R)

ATROPINE
Antidote: Physostigmine (R)

ANTICOAGULANTS
Antidote: vitamin K (R)

3 Chemical incident inquiry form

These will probably be generated by the local authority, but a sample form is given below.

Call received by _____ Position _____

Date _____ Time _____

Informant details

Name _____

Position _____

Address _____

Contact numbers _____

Incident details

Type of event (see list below) _____

Date _____ Time _____

Type of premises _____

Company _____

Address _____

Postcode _____

Tel. number _____

Further information _____

Type of Event

Fire   State of combustion in which inflammable material burns, producing heat, flames and often smoke.

Explosion   Violent release of energy resulting from a rapid chemical reaction, especially one that produces shock wave, loud noise, heat and light.

Waste   Inappropriate or unauthorised disposal of waste products, both domestic and industrial; seepage of waste products from waste disposal site to an adjacent site lead to comtamination.

Water   Contamination of drinking water, oceans, rivers, lakes, estuaries, ground water etc.

Food & drink   Contamination of any substance containing nutrients, such as carbohydrates, proteins and fats that is ingested for the purpose of generating energy and body tissue.

Medicine   Contamination of substances that are used to restore or preserve health.

Malicious act   Act motivated by wrongful, vicious or mischievious purpose.

Air   Contamination of the gases that we normally breathe.

Leak   Crack, hole or fault in a container or pipe leading to a release of material. Carbon monoxide exposures from blocked flues or faulty systems can be inserted here.

Spill   Act of disgorging contents from a container unintentionally.

Transport accident   Unforeseen event involving a vehicle used to transport goods or people.

Land   Contamination of the land surface of the earth that is composed of disintegrated rock particles, humus, water and air.

Information about casualties or exposed persons and their management

Exposed

Symptomatic

Casualties

Deaths

Weather conditions (Please give details of prevailing conditions, e.g. dry, overcast, windy with direction if known)

Information from CHEMET

Further action needed initially

Yes ☐   No ☐   If no, why not?

If Yes,   has a major incident been declared? Yes ☐   No ☐

If Yes,   When?

by Whom?

Position? _____

Meet at _____

Date _____

Time _____

Lead person

Name _____

Organisation _____

Position _____

Contact number _____

Chemical substances involved

Substance 1

Name(s) _____

Confirmed/suspected? _____

Amount (kg) _____

UN No. _____

Manufacturer CAS No. _____

Physical state of chemical _____

Radioactive?   Yes ☐   No ☐

Affecting air/water/food/soil/not known/other (please specify)?

_____

Toxicology requested?   Yes ☐   No ☐

Verbal info. obtained?   Yes ☐   No ☐

Faxed/written info. obtained?   Yes ☐   No ☐

Substance 2

Name(s) _____

Confirmed/suspected? _____

Amount (kg) _____

UN No. _____

Manufacturer CAS No.

Physical state of chemical

Radioactive?   Yes ☐ No ☐

Affecting air/water/food/soil/not known/other (please specify)?

Toxicology requested?   Yes ☐ No ☐

Verbal info. obtained?   Yes ☐ No ☐

Faxed/written info. obtained? Yes ☐ No ☐

Substance 3

Name(s)

Confirmed/suspected?

Amount (kg)

UN No.

Manufacturer CAS No.

Physical state of chemical

Radioactive?   Yes ☐ No ☐

Affecting air/water/food/soil/not known/other (please specify)?

Toxicology requested?   Yes ☐ No ☐

Verbal info. obtained?   Yes ☐ No ☐

Faxed/written info. obtained? Yes ☐ No ☐

Substance 4

Name(s)

Confirmed/suspected?

Amount (kg)

UN No.

Manufacturer CAS No.

Physical state of chemical

Radioactive? Yes ☐ No ☐

Affecting air/water/food/soil/not known/other (please specify)?

_____

Toxicology requested? Yes ☐ No ☐

Verbal info. obtained? Yes ☐ No ☐

Faxed/written info. obtained? Yes ☐ No ☐

_____

Continuing action needed? Yes ☐ No ☐ If No, why not?

_____

Action _check list_

Detailed log

Refer to local major incident plan

Incident control team

_____

Liaison (note name of contact, contact number, date, time and reason for contact):

Organisation/dept.

Emergency services

Fire

Police

Ambulance

Health authority

CCDC

DPH

EPO

GM

Clerical

Media

Other 1

Other 2

_____

Trust

A/E

Medical director

Occ. health

Primary care

GP

Local authority

EHO

HEPO

DoH

CMO

Specialist centres

Chemical incident adviser

NPIS

SCIEH

National Focus

HAGGCI

Voluntary agencies

Others

Continuing action needed?   Yes ☐ No ☐   If No, why not?

Check Clinical Provision:

- Check provision of emergency services.
- Redirect other casualties.
- Set up decontamination facilities.
- Notify and request assistance from neighbouring authority.

Continuing action needed?   Yes ☐   No ☐   If No, why not?

_____

_____

Advice to public?   Yes ☐   No ☐   Deferred ☐

Date required _____   Time required _____

Method _____

Press statement ☐   Leaflet ☐   Vans ☐   GP ☐   Other(s) ☐

Protection of public

Is a decision on sheltering/evacuation needed?   Yes ☐   No ☐

Has it been made?   Yes ☐   No ☐

What was it? _____

Zone description _____

Time _____

Who made it? _____

Name _____

Position _____

Contact no. _____

How is it being issued? _____

Health care provision _____

Assessment of Acute Health Effects _____

Clinical provision checklist

• Provision of emergency services
• Redirection of other casualties
• Set up decontamination facilities
• Notify and request assistance from neighbouring authority

Epidemiological assessment of those exposed

Initiate register of:

- demographic details
- where attended: site/work/hospital/GP/community centre/other (specify)
- exposure status
- high–risk groups
- symptoms
- signs
- clinical tests
- sampling
- analysis

Environmental

Areas to be considered:

Environmental sampling

Food ☐ Water ☐ Air ☐ Soil ☐ Vegetation ☐ Animals ☐

Consultation: further investigation and follow–up

- public
- scientists
- industry
- politicians

Keeping affected community informed

- follow–up
- debrief – hot/planned

Psychological intervention

Assessment made?   Yes ☐ No ☐

Required   Yes ☐ No ☐

Audit

- lessons learned
- plan publication
- 1st author

4 Questionnaire for use in follow-up studies

Date _____

Section 1   Personal details

1.1   Surname _____

1.2   First names _____

1.3   Home address (please include postcode) _____

_____

_____

_____

_____ Postcode _____

Tel. _____

1.4   Date of birth _____

1.5   Sex?   Male (Go to Q1.9) ☐   Female (Go to Q1.6) ☐

1.6   Are you pregnant?   Yes (Go to Q1.7) ☐   No (Go to Q1.9) ☐

1.7   Date of last menstrual period? (If you can't remember, go to Q 1.8)

_____

1.8   When is your baby due? _____

1.9   Occupation _____

1.10   Employer's address (please include postcode)

_____

_____

_____

_____ Postcode _____

Tel. _____

1.11   GP's name _____

1.12   GP's address (please include postcode)

_____

_____

_____ Postcode _____

Tel. _____

Section 2   **Exposure details**

2.1   Date of incident

2.2   Time of incident _____   AM/PM (delete as appropriate)

2.3   Was there a:

- gas cloud?   ☐

- dust cloud?   ☐

- liquid spillage?   ☐

- other (please specify)?   ☐

        Other: _____

2.4   Where were you at the time of the incident?

- At work?   ☐

- At home?   ☐

- Elsewhere (please specify location)?   ☐

        Elsewhere: _____

2.5   Were you:

- indoors   ☐

- outdoors   ☐

2.6   Degree of exposure★

2.7   Duration of exposure★

        Short (less than 10 minutes)   ☐

        Medium (10–30 minutes)   ☐

        Long (greater than 30 minutes)   ☐

(★Criteria to be decided at time of incident)

2.8   Other relevant details (e.g. was protective clothing worn)?

Section 3   Previous medical history

3.1   Do you suffer from any chronic diseases?   Yes (Go to Q3.2) ☐

No (Go to Q3.3) ☐

3.2   What do you suffer from?

- chronic chest complaints? ☐
- asthma? ☐
- bronchitis? ☐
- other chest condition (please specify)? ☐

Other chest conditions: _____

- Diabetes? ☐
- Rheumatism/arthritis? ☐
- Heart disease? ☐
- Other (please specify)? ☐

Other: _____

3.3   Do you take any regular medication? No ☐ Yes (please specify) ☐

_____

_____

3.4   Have you ever suffered from any of the following problems?

- high blood pressure ☐
- migraine/headaches ☐
- anxiety/depression ☐
- abdominal pains/diarrhoea ☐
- skin problems ☐

3.5   Have you had any illness within the last six weeks?

No ☐   Yes (please specify) ☐

_____

_____

_____

3.6   Do you smoke?

    • Never   ☐ (Go to Q3.12)

    • Used to   ☐ (Go to Q3.7)

    • Yes   ☐ (Go to Q3.10)

3.7   When did you last smoke? _____

3.8   How long did you smoke?   months/years (delete as appropriate)

3.9   What amount per day did you smoke? _____

3.10   How long have you smoked?   months/years (delete as appropriate)

3.11   What amount per day do you smoke? _____

3.12   Do you drink alcohol regularly?

    • non drinker   ☐

    • less than 1 unit/week   ☐

    • 1 or more units/week (please specify)   ☐

    (No. of units) _____

Section 4   Current state of health

4.1   Do you have any unusual symptoms at present?   Yes (Go to Q4.2) ☐

    No (Go to Q4.6) ☐

4.2   What are these symptoms?

    1 _____

    2 _____

    3 _____

4.3   When did each symptom start?

    1 _____

    2 _____

    3 _____

4.4   Have you consulted anyone about them?   Yes (Go to Q4.5) ☐

    No (Go to Q4.6) ☐

4.5   Who have you consulted?

    _____

    _____

4.6   How do you rate your overall health at present?

(Please mark the line between the crosses where it is most appropriate for you.)

X_____X

As bad as it could be   Perfect health

4.7   How anxious are you at present about your health?

(Please mark the line between the crosses where it is most appropriate for you.)

X_____X

I worry all the time   No worries at all

4.8   Is there anything else important that you think we should know?

_____

_____

_____

4.9   Do you give us your permission to obtain relevant medical information

relating to you?   Yes (Go to 4.10) ☐   No   ☐

4.10   I give permission for my doctors to provide the Department of Public
Health, ...

Health Authority with relevant medical information relating to myself.

SIGNED _____

PLEASE PRINT NAME _____

Date _____

Thank you very much for your help.

In case of queries, or for more advice, please contact ....

5 Questionnaire

Questionnaire for those attending a reception centre after a nuclear emergency is declared

Reception centre ID

1. Name:

2. Address:

Postcode

Tel.

3. Age: years/months (delete as appropriate)

4. Sex?   Male (Go to Q7) ☐   Female (Go to Q5) ☐

5. If female, do you know if you are pregnant: Yes (Go to Q6) ☐

No (Go to Q7) ☐

6. When is the baby due?

7. Time of arrival at reception centre:

8. Are you receiving medical attention?   Yes (Go to Q9) ☐

No (Go to Q10) ☐

9. If Yes, please give details:

10. GP's name:

11. GP's address:

Postcode

Tel.

THIS SECTION TO BE COMPLETED BY NHS PERSONNEL

Contaminated?   Yes ☐   No ☐

Potassium iodate tablets given?   Yes ☐   No ☐

If Yes, dose: 2 tablets ☐   1 tablet ☐   ½ tablet ☐

If No, were there contra-indications?   Yes ☐   No ☐

If Yes, which: Dermatitis herpetiformis ☐

                                Hypocomplementaemic vasculitis ☐

6 Cluster initial contact information sheet

Caller data

Name of caller:

Address of caller:

Postcode:

Tel

Organisation (if any) to which caller is linked

Cluster data

Suspected health event(s) (If cancer, generic or of specific site?)

Suspected exposure(s) (relate purported exposure to health event)

Number of cases

Geographical area of concern

Time period

How caller became aware of problem

Personal information on people allegedly affected by health event

This information may be collected over a number of contacts with different people.

Name of affected person _____

Address of affected person _____

_____

_____

_____ Postcode _____

Tel _____

Sex of affected person _____

Age/date of birth of affected person _____

Length of time at home address _____

Specific occupation of affected person _____

_____

Employer of affected person (if known) _____

_____

_____

Clinical complaint(s) _____

_____

_____

_____

Diagnosis _____

_____

Date of diagnosis _____

Date of death (if applicable) _____

Exposure location (if different from address) _____

Length of time at exposure location _____

Contact person for exposed person _____

_____

Relationship to exposed person _____

_____

Contact details

GP of affected person

GP's address

GP's tel.

Consultant of affected person

Unit

Additional information

Discuss impressions with the caller, stressing a number of important points as appropriate:

- A variety of diagnoses is not suggestive of a common origin.
- Cancer is common (1 in 4 lifetime risk). This increases with age (cases among older people less likely to be true cluster) and with activities such as tobacco smoking.
- Cancers affecting a specific site imply more potential for there being a cluster, especially if they are rare cancers.
- Major birth defects are less common than cancer but do occur in 1–2% of live births.
- Length of time in residence/at exposure location would have to be substantial to implicate a plausible carcinogen due to long latent period of most known carcinogens before they exert an effect.
- Purported fatal exposures/cases may not prove helpful as there will be a lack of information on exposure and possible confounding factors.
- Even if rare diseases do cluster and appear to be statistically significant, this may be a statistical phenomenon unrelated to any exposure.
- Assure caller he/she will receive a written response.

7 Decontamination facilities

The government has laid down standards for decontamination facilities.[1] The following features are considered to be basic.

The designated decontamination room must not be used for any other purpose.

It may take the form of a temporary building (or a number of these) purpose-built for showering. Such structures can be held centrally at a supra-district or regional level and transported to the relevant hospital(s) when required. These facilities should ideally be able to store contaminated water for later safe disposal under advice from the environmental health department and the water authorities.

The room should have its own access from outside the unit to allow patients to enter, and separate access into the unit, similar to the 'clean' and 'dirty' areas in an operating theatre.

The room should have its own ventilation system.

Showering facilities should be available for both ambulatory and non–ambulatory patients. A fixed shower nozzle may be adequate for patients who are able to sit or stand, but not those confined to a trolley. A new decontamination couch has been designed at the Christie Hospital NHS Trust to overcome this problem and is currently being considered by several A&E departments throughout the country. The couch can be attached to a standard trolley, has a hose and spray attachment which can be connected to the mains, and includes a 50 litre capacity drum to collect run-off water for disposal or analysis.

A hosepipe which can be run outside will enable decontamination of people outside the A&E department, avoiding contaminating it. It may be necessary to request the fire service to allow you to use one of their holding tanks for the contaminated water. Fuller's earth should be available to mop up spillages.

Clear, double plastic sacks should be available for disposal of clothing. Seal them tightly, label them clearly and place them outside the department in a secure, clearly signed store in order to prevent theft of contents, breakage or inadvertant refuse collection. If possible and safe, it is a good idea to retrieve essential personal belongings before disposing of the clothing.

Guidance on protective clothing for staff and related standards is expected.

Provision of protective clothing varies considerably in different A&E departments, and it is not unusual to find that the only equipment available is plastic aprons and standard-issue surgical gloves.

Some health authorities have sought specific guidance in planning their response. Risk assessments should take account of the Personal Protective Equipment at Work Regulations 1992 and guidance from British Standards documents including BS 7184 (1989), *The Selection, Use and Maintenance of Chemical Protective Clothing* and BS 4275 (1974), *The Selection, Use and Maintenance of Respiratory Protective Equipment.*

The equipment which may be required includes an oversuit with integral hood and feet offering a two to six-hour chemical breakthrough time, gloves covering the wrist offering high performance in resisting permeation and penetration, goggles and a respirator with both a dust and multi-filter.

The suggested absolute minimum of protective equipment is:

- a long rubber apron
- wellington boots as in the operating theatre
- goggles
- gloves of reasonably heavy rubber

A&E department staff handling or disposing of potentially contaminated urine, vomitus, etc. should wear protective clothing, and arrangements should be in place for separate disposal of materials marked with warning labels.

There will also be a need to provide information and advice to members of the public who have been exposed to toxins.

[1] Department of Health and Social Services (1988) *Health Building Note 22: Accident and Emergency Department*, HBN 22 1988, London: DHSS.

8 Telecom Alphabet

A   ALPHA

B   BRAVO

C   CHARLIE

D   DELTA

E   ECHO

F   FOXTROT

G   GOLF

H   HOTEL

I   INDIA

J   JULIET

K   KILO

L   LIMA

M   MIKE

N   NOVEMBER

O   OSCAR

P   PAPA

Q   QUEBEC

R   ROMEO

S   SIERRA

T   TANGO

U   UNIFORM

V   VICTOR

W   WHISKY

X   X-RAY

Y   YANKEE

Z   ZULU

Bibliography

General

Roueché, B. (1991), *The Medical Detectives*, Truman Tally Books/Plume, Penguin Books.

Antidotes

London: British Medical Association/Royal Pharmaceutical Society of Great Britain, *British National Formulary*.

Meredith, T.J. (1994), *Evaluation of Antidote Volume 2*: Antidotes for Poisoning by Cyanide. Cambridge: Cambridge University Press.

Meredith, T.J. (1995), *Evaluation of Antidote Volume 3*: Antidotes for Poisoning by Paracetamol. Cambridge: Cambridge University Press.

Meredith, T.J., Jacobsen, D., Haines, J.A and Berger, J.C. (1993), *Evaluation of Antidote Volume 1*: Naloxone, flumenazil and dantrolene as Antidotes, Cambridge: Cambridge University Press.

Epidemiology

Clusters

Anon. (1990) 'Disease clustering: Hide or seek', *Lancet* **336,** pp.717–18.

Anon. (1990) 'National conference on clustering of health events, Atlanta, Georgia, February 1989', *American Journal of Epidemiology*, **132,** supplement No. 1.

Centers for Disease Control and Prevention (1990) 'Guidelines for investigating clusters of health events', *Morbidity and Mortality Weekly Report*, **39** (RR-11) pp.1–23.

Elliott, P. (ed.) 1989 *Methodology of Enquiries into Disease Clustering*, London: Small Area Health Statistics Unit.

Olsen S.F., Martuzzi, M. and Elliott, P. (1996) 'Cluster analysis and disease mapping – why, when, and how? A step by step guide'. *Britsh Medical Journal*, **313,** pp.863–6.

Environmental epidemiology

Aldrich, T., Griffith, J. and Cooke, C. (1993) *Environmental Epidemiology and Risk Assessment*. New York: Van Nostrand Reinhold.

Lawrence, J. (1988) *Report of an Inquiry into an Incident at Lowermoor Water Treatment Works of South West Water Authority on 6 July 1988*. Brixham: CIC Brixham Laboratory.

Lowermoor Incident Health Advisory Group (1989) *Water Pollution at Lowermoor, North Cornwall*, London: HMSO.

Lowermoor Incident Health Advisory Group (1991) *Water Pollution at Lowermoor, North Cornwall (Second Report)*, London: HMSO.

Surveillance

Hertz-Picciotto, I. (1996) 'Comment: Toward a coordinated system for the surveillance of environmental health hazards', *American Journal of Public Health*, **86**(5), pp.638–41.

Thacker, S.B., Stroup, D.F., Parrish, R.G. and Anderson, H.A. (1996) 'Surveillance in environmental public health: issues, systems, and sources', *American Journal of Public Health*, **86**(5), pp.633–8.

Radiation

Chief Medical Officer (1993) *Potassium iodate (stable iodine) prophylaxis in the event of a nuclear incident*, PL/CMO(93)1, London: Department of Health.

Department of Health (1991) *Report on Health and Social Subjects 39. Nuclear Accident Countermeasures: Iodine Prophylaxis. Report of the United Kingdom Working Group on Iodine Prophylaxis following Nuclear Accidents*, London: HMSO.

Health and Safety Executive (1994) *Arrangements for Responding to Nuclear Emergencies*, London: HMSO.

International Atomic Energy Agency (1996) *International Basic Safety Standards for Protection Against Ionising Radiation and for the Safety of Radiation Sources, Safety Standards series No. 115*, Vienna: IAEA.

World Health Organisation (1989) *Nuclear accidents: Harmonisation of the Public Health Response*, European Reports and Studies 110, Copenhagen: WHO.

World Health Organisation (1994) *Manual on Public Health Action in Radiation Emergencies*, European Centre for Environment and Health, Rome Division, WHO.

Clinical toxicology

Wetherall, D.J., Ledingham, J.G.G. and Warrell, D.A. (1996) *Oxford Textbook of Medicine* (3rd edition), Oxford: Oxford University Press.

When using books and databases from the USA, it is necessary to be aware that clinical practice may differ with respect to dosages and/or specific antidotes.

All the following have a useful clinical or environmental emphasis and have been grouped into three price ranges and classified by specialisation (B = basic handbook, T = more advanced textbook, M = specialist monograph).

Price <£50

MAFF & HSE (1996) *Pesticides*, London: HMSO. (B)

Olson, K.R. (1998) *Poisoning and Drug Overdose* (3rd edn), London: Prentice Hall. Useful at handbook level, well organised, includes section on emergency response to chemical incidents. (B)

Timbrell, J.A. (1991) *Principles of Biochemical Toxicology* (2nd edn), London: Taylor and Francis. Highly recommended as an introduction. (B)

Price £50–£100

Ballantyne, B., Marrs, T. and Turner, P. (1995) *General and Applied Toxicology* (abridged edn), London: Macmillan. (T)

Baselt, R.C. and Cravey, R.C. (1996) *Disposition of Toxic Drugs and Chemicals in Man*, (4th edn), Foster City California: Chemical Toxicology Institute. Refers to the pharmacology of chemicals. (M)

Hathaway, G.J., Proctor, N.H. and Hughes, J.P. (1996) *Chemical Hazards of the Workplace.* (4th edn), New York: Van Nostrand Reinhold. Includes a table of physical clues to occupational poisoning.(M)

Price £101–200

Ellenhorn, M.J. (1996) *Ellenhorn's Medical Toxicology: Diagnosis and Treatment of Human Poisoning* (2nd edn), Baltimore: Williams & Wilkins. (T)

Goldfrank, L.R. (1994) *Goldfrank's Toxicologic Emergencies* (5th edn), Norwalk, Connecticut: Prentice-Hall. (T)

Reynolds, J.E.F. (1996) *Martindale: The Extra Pharmacopoeia* (31st edition), London: The Pharmaceutical Press. Includes UK trade names, and some chemicals and antiseptics; also available on-line. (M)

Sullivan, J.B. (1992) *Hazardous Materials Toxicology: Clinical Principles of Environmental Health*, Baltimore: Williams & Wilkins. (T)

Price >£200

Dollery, C. (1998) *Therapeutic Drugs* (2 vols), Edinburgh: Churchill Livingstone. Comprehensive monographs on many drugs. (M)

Grant, W.M. (1994) *Toxicology of the Eye.* (4th edn), Springfield, Illinois: Thomas. (T)

Index

Printed in the United Kingdom for The Stationery Office   J57648   CI0   04/99   10170